First Step Arabic

Read & Write 200+ Words with Short & Long Vowels Independently

Nisreen Neqresh Beshqoy

First Step Arabic
Read & Write 200+ Words
With Short & Long Vowels Independently

Published by Nisreen Neqresh Beshqoy
Edits by Natalia Beshqoy
Graphic Design by Noor Beshqoy

Paperback ISBN: 979-8-9906707-0-9
Library of Congress Control Number: 2024923762

Arabic Fundamentals:

Your Study Guide to Success

Welcome to First Step Arabic! Before you dive into the exciting world of Arabic vocabulary, it's essential to grasp the foundational principles outlined in the study guide ahead. These guidelines offer key insights into Arabic script, pronunciation, and vowel usage, serving as your roadmap to mastering reading and writing the Arabic alphabet with both long and short vowels. Refer back to these pages whenever you need guidance—they lay the groundwork for your Arabic learning journey.

STUDY GUIDE

Arabic Alphabet Overview:

- The Arabic alphabet consists of 28 letters.
- Arabic is read and written from right to left.

خ	ح	ج	ث	ت	ب	أ
ḳhaa	ḥaa	jeem	thaa	taa	baa	alif
ص	ش	س	ز	ر	ذ	د
ṣaad	sheen	seen	zay	raa	dhaal	daal
ق	ف	غ	ع	ظ	ط	ض
q̣aaf	faa	g̣hayn	ʿayn	ḍhaa	ṭaa	ḍaad
ي	و	هـ	ن	م	ل	ك
yaa	waw	haa	noon	meem	laam	kaaf

How Arabic Script Works:

- The Arabic script is cursive, with letters connecting to form words. Each letter changes shape depending on its position in a word (beginning, middle, end, or isolated).
- All Arabic letters are consonants and have a 'still' sound on their own. To achieve a complete or 'full' sound, they require vowels. Vowels work alongside consonants to form words, highlighting the collaborative nature of Arabic script.

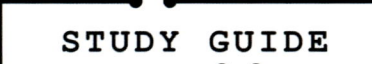

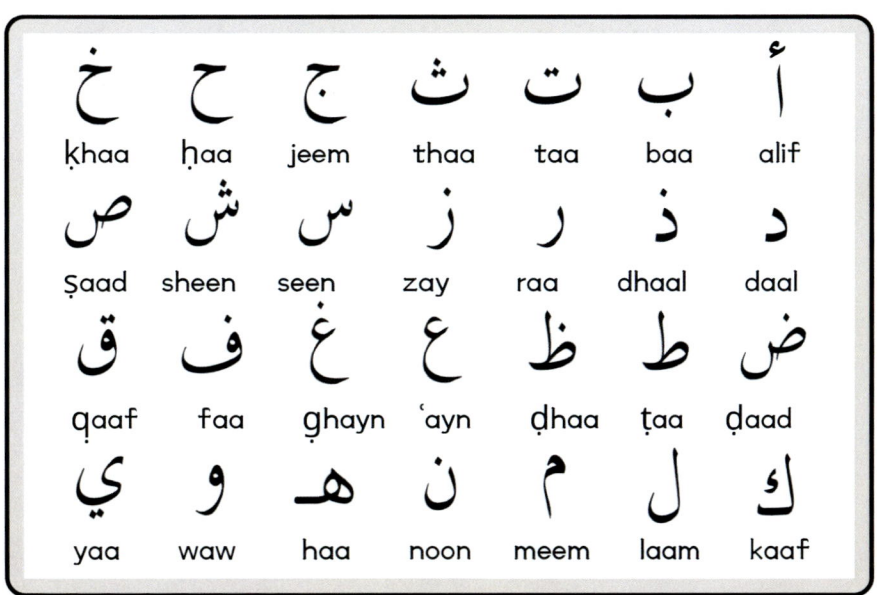

STUDY GUIDE

The Use of Modern Standard Arabic (MSA) in This Book

- This book uses words derived from commonly spoken Modern Standard Arabic (MSA), avoiding reliance on specific dialects or the highly formal Classical Arabic found in other resources.

Understanding Vowels in Arabic:

- Arabic has three long vowels and three short vowels.
- Short vowels, known as Harakat (meaning 'movement' in Arabic), are marks placed above or below consonants to indicate vowel sounds.
- Long vowels are part of the Arabic alphabet. When acting as long vowels, they extend the sound length of their short vowel counterparts, elongating the pronunciation of the preceding letter. They can also function as regular consonants.

Short Vowels:

- Short vowels in Arabic play a crucial role in pronunciation and are represented by diacritic marks. They are much shorter in duration than long vowels. The three short vowels in Arabic are:

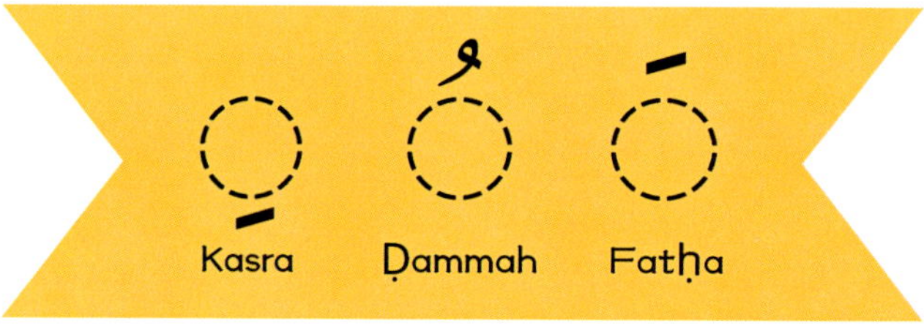

1. Fatḥa
   - Pronounced as "a"
   - Corresponds to the long vowel (ا) alif pronounced “aa”
2. Ḍammah
   - Pronounced as "o"
   - Corresponds to the long vowel (و) waw pronounced “oo”
3. Kasra
   - Pronounced as "i"
   - Corresponds to the long vowel (ي) yaa pronounced “ee”

Long Vowels:

- In Arabic, a long vowel typically lasts twice as long as its corresponding short vowel. The long vowels in Arabic are:

ي	و	ا
Yaa	Waw	Alif

1. **Alif**
   - Pronounced as "aa"
   - Corresponds to the short vowel (Fatḥa) pronounced “a”
2. **Waw**
   - Pronounced as "oo"
   - Corresponds to the short vowel (Ḍammah) pronounced “o”
3. **Yaa**
   - Pronounced as "ee"
   - Corresponds to the short vowel (Kasra) pronounced “i”

The Importance of Vowel Pronunciation

- In both written and spoken Modern Standard Arabic (MSA), pronouncing vowels at the end of words is not essential for conveying meaning but primarily serves grammatical purposes, especially in classical texts.
- However, accurately pronouncing vowels at the beginning and middle of words is crucial for clarity and correct pronunciation.

English Vowels Correspondence:

- In this book's English pronunciation system, single vowels (a, o, i) represent Arabic short vowels, while double vowels (aa, oo, ee) represent Arabic long vowels. Long vowels are pronounced for about twice the duration of short vowels.

One-Way Connectors:

- There are six one-way connector letters in Arabic that join the preceding letter in a word but do not connect to the following letter. As a result, any letter that follows these six connectors takes its isolated or beginning form. These one-way connector letters are:

و - waw	ز - zay	ر - raa	ذ - dhaal	د - daal	أ - alif

Emphatic Deep Sound Letters:

- In this book, English letters with a dot underneath represent the nine Arabic deep-sound letters, which are pronounced from deep in the mouth or throat.
- While most Arabic letters produce frontal sounds like English, nine letters stand out for their very deep pronunciation, four of which have no English equivalent.

ق - qaf	غ - ghayn	ع - ʿayn	ظ - ḍhaa	ط - ṭaa	ض - ḍaad	ص - ṣaad	خ - ḳhaa	ح - ḥaa

1. ح - ḥaa

Pronounced from the depths of the throat, similar to the sound produced when clearing the lower throat or softly coughing (no English equivalent).

2. خ - ḳhaa

Pronounced from deep in the throat, similar to the sound made when clearing the upper throat (no English equivalent).

3. ص - ṣaad

Pronounced like the 'S' in 'sun' and 'subway,' but with added depth and emphasis, produced by pressing the tongue lower in the mouth.

4. ض - ḍaad

Pronounced like the 'D' in 'done' and 'double,' but with greater emphasis, produced by pressing the tongue against the upper gums.

5. ط - ṭaa

Pronounced like the 'T' in 'ton' and 'but,' but with stronger emphasis, produced by pressing the tongue against the roof of the mouth.

6. ظ - ḍhaa

Pronounced like the 'TH' in 'mother' and 'father,' but with stronger emphasis, produced by pressing the tongue against the upper teeth.

7. ع - ʿayn

Begin by saying 'A' while pressing your tongue downward. The sound is produced deep in the throat, similar to the effort of lifting something heavy (no English equivalent).

8. غ - ghayn

Produced from the upper part of the throat, resembling a gargling sound, similar to the French 'R' but stronger and more pronounced (no English equivalent).

9. ق - qaaf

Pronounced like a deeper, stronger 'K' sound, produced from the back of the throat with more emphasis than the English 'C' in 'come' and 'column.'

Arabic Diacritics:

- The 'Sukoon' signifies 'stillness' and represents a consonant without a vowel sound. It appears as a small circle above the letter.
- The 'Shaddah' indicates the doubling of the letter's sound, signifying 'intensity.' It appears as a miniature 'w' shape above the letter.

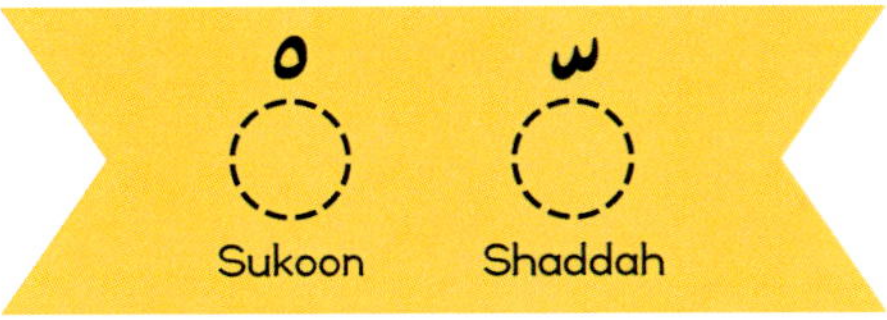

The Maddah Symbol with Alif: Usage and Rules

- When 'Alif Hamza'—which refers to Alif functioning as a regular consonant—is followed by another 'Alif Hamza' (أأ) or a long vowel Alif (أا), instead of writing the letter twice, it is written as a single Alif (آ) with a 'Maddah' (ٓ) symbol on top.
- The Maddah (ٓ) appears as a small curved line resembling a wave placed above the first Alif, indicating the elongation of the Alif Hamza sound.

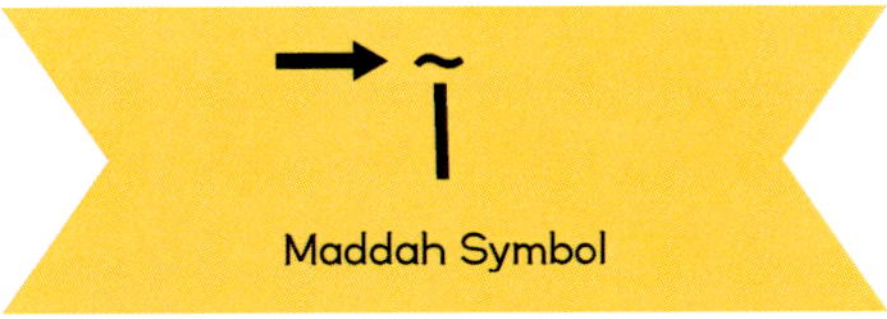

Masculine and Feminine Classification:

- In Arabic, words are classified as either masculine or feminine. Masculine words do not have specific signs, whereas feminine words often follow recognizable signs.
- One common way to identify feminine words is through the most common feminine marker, known as the closed 'T' (ة). This form is derived from the regular 'T' (ت) and is used to indicate femininity. It is pronounced like a regular 'Ta'.
- In written Modern Standard Arabic, the closed 'T' (ة) is used, but it is not commonly pronounced in speech. However, in Classical Arabic, particularly in contexts such as poetry and the Quran, it is fully pronounced.
- The 'Fatḥa' vowel (َ◌), which sounds like 'a,' always appears just before the closed 'T' (ة) and is consistently pronounced. Hearing the 'Fatḥa' at the end of a noun or adjective often indicates that the word is feminine.
- The closed 'T' appears as (ة) when preceded by a one-way connector letter and as (ـة) when preceded by a two-way connector letter.
- Unlike feminine words, masculine words do not have specific markers to indicate their gender.

The Pronunciation:
Arabic Alphabet with Short & Long Vowels

STUDY GUIDE

Long Vowels			Short Vowels			
Yaa (ee)	Waw (oo)	Alif (aa)	Kasra (i)	Ḍammah (o)	Fatḥa (a)	Alphabet Name
إي	أو	آ	إِ	أُ	أَ	Alif
ee	oo	aa	i	o	a	
بي	بو	با	بِ	بُ	بَ	Baa
bee	boo	baa	bi	bo	ba	
تي	تو	تا	تِ	تُ	تَ	Taa
tee	too	taa	ti	to	ta	
ثي	ثو	ثا	ثِ	ثُ	ثَ	Thaa
thee	thoo	thaa	thi	tho	tha	
جي	جو	جا	جِ	جُ	جَ	Jeem
jee	joo	jaa	ji	jo	ja	
حي	حو	حا	حِ	حُ	حَ	Ḥaa
ḥee	ḥoo	ḥaa	ḥi	ḥo	ḥa	
خي	خو	خا	خِ	خُ	خَ	Ḳhaa
ḳhee	ḳhoo	ḳhaa	ḳhi	ḳho	ḳha	
دي	دو	دا	دِ	دُ	دَ	Daal
dee	doo	daa	di	do	da	
ذي	ذو	ذا	ذِ	ذُ	ذَ	Dhaal
dhee	dhoo	dhaa	dhi	dho	dha	
ري	رو	را	رِ	رُ	رَ	Raa
ree	roo	raa	ri	ro	ra	
زي	زو	زا	زِ	زُ	زَ	Zay
zee	zoo	zaa	zi	zo	za	
سي	سو	سا	سِ	سُ	سَ	Seen
see	soo	saa	si	so	sa	
شي	شو	شا	شِ	شُ	شَ	Sheen
shee	shoo	shaa	shi	sho	sha	
صي	صو	صا	صِ	صُ	صَ	Ṣaad
ṣee	ṣoo	ṣaa	ṣi	ṣo	ṣa	

Long Vowels			Short Vowels			Alphabet Name
Yaa (ee)	Waw (oo)	Alif (aa)	Kasra (i)	Ḍammah (o)	Fatḥa (a)	
ضي	ضو	ضا	ضِ	ضُ	ضَ	Ḍaad
ḍee	ḍoo	ḍaa	ḍi	ḍo	ḍa	
طي	طو	طا	طِ	طُ	طَ	Ṭaa
ṭee	ṭoo	ṭaa	ṭi	ṭo	ṭa	
ظي	ظو	ظا	ظِ	ظُ	ظَ	Ḍhaa
ḍhee	ḍhoo	ḍhaa	ḍhi	ḍho	ḍha	
عي	عو	عا	عِ	عُ	عَ	ʿAyn
ʿee	ʿoo	ʿaa	ʿi	ʿo	ʿa	
غي	غو	غا	غِ	غُ	غَ	Ghayn
ghee	ghoo	ghaa	ghi	gho	gha	
في	فو	فا	فِ	فُ	فَ	Faa
fee	foo	faa	fi	fo	fa	
قي	قو	قا	قِ	قُ	قَ	Qaaf
qee	qoo	qaa	qi	qo	qa	
كي	كو	كا	كِ	كُ	كَ	Kaaf
kee	koo	kaa	ki	ko	ka	
لي	لو	لا	لِ	لُ	لَ	Laam
lee	loo	laa	li	lo	la	
مي	مو	ما	مِ	مُ	مَ	Meem
mee	moo	maa	mi	mo	ma	
ني	نو	نا	نِ	نُ	نَ	Noon
nee	noo	naa	ni	no	na	
هي	هو	ها	هِ	هُ	هَ	Haa
hee	hoo	haa	hi	ho	ha	
وي	وو	وا	وِ	وُ	وَ	Waw
wee	woo	waa	wi	wo	wa	
يي	يو	يا	يِ	يُ	يَ	Yaa
yee	yoo	yaa	yi	yo	ya	

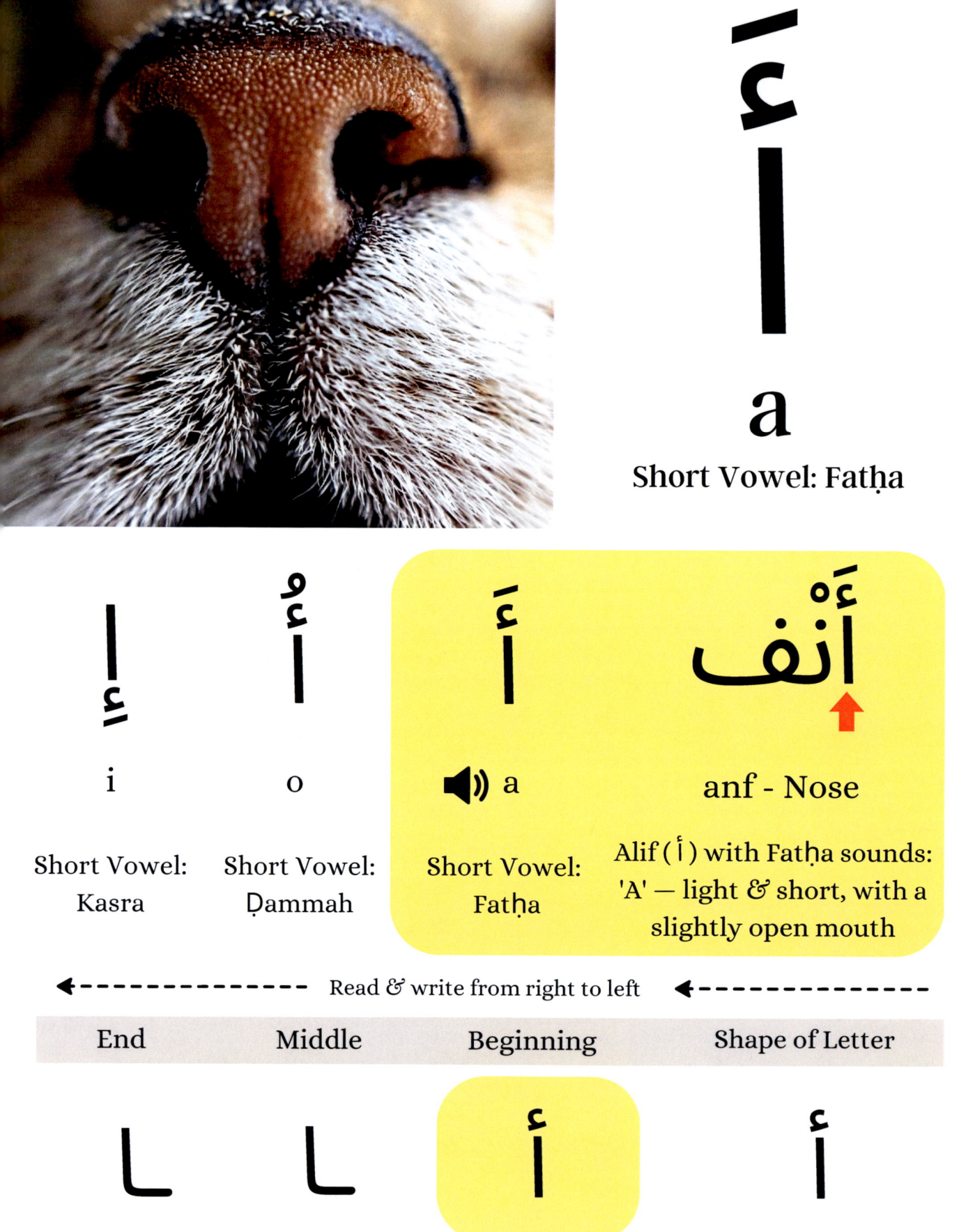

أَ

a

Short Vowel: Fatḥa

أَنْف

anf - Nose

Alif (أ) with Fatḥa sounds: 'A' — light & short, with a slightly open mouth

أَ	أُ	إِ
a	o	i
Short Vowel: Fatḥa	Short Vowel: Ḍammah	Short Vowel: Kasra

Read & write from right to left

Shape of Letter	Beginning	Middle	End
أ	أ	ـأ	ـأ

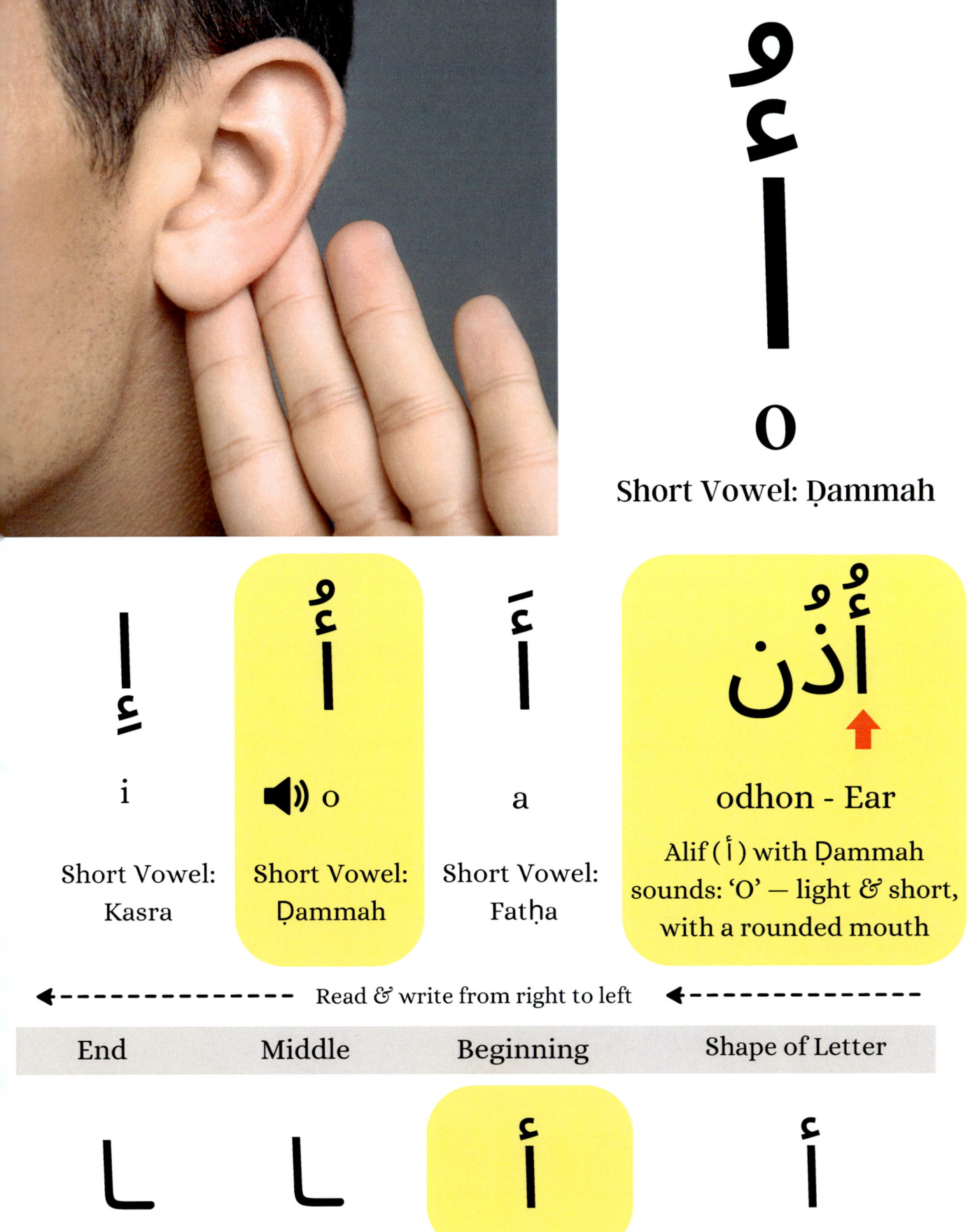

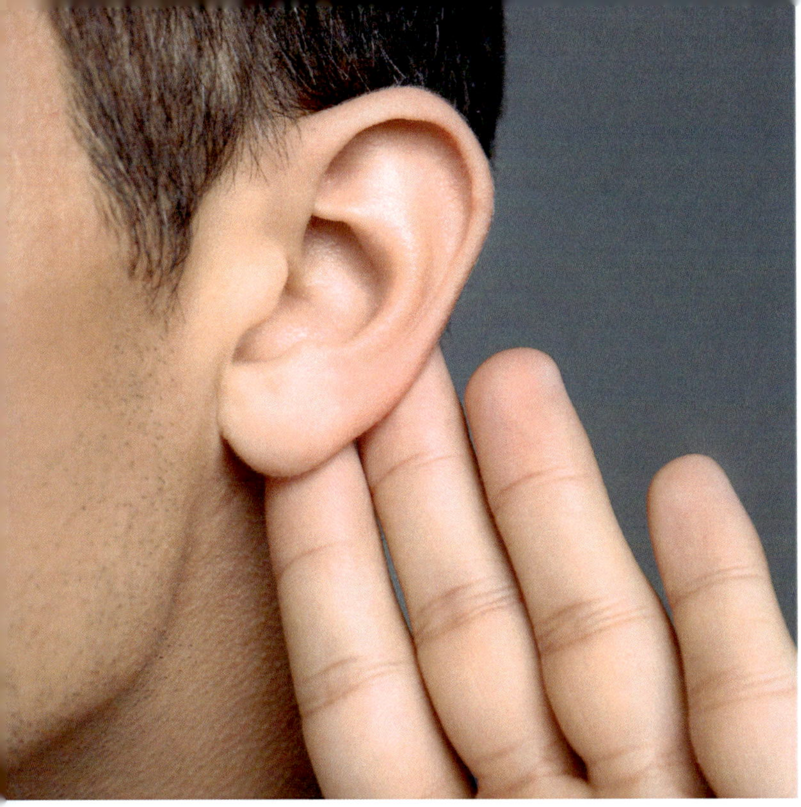

أُ

o

Short Vowel: Ḍammah

إِ	أُ	أَ	أُذُن
i	o	a	odhon - Ear
Short Vowel: Kasra	Short Vowel: Ḍammah	Short Vowel: Fatḥa	Alif (أ) with Ḍammah sounds: 'O' — light & short, with a rounded mouth

Read & write from right to left

End	Middle	Beginning	Shape of Letter
ـا	ـا	أ	أ

إِـا

i

Short Vowel: Kasra

ـِا	ـُا	ـَا	إِبْتِسَامَة
i	o	a	ibtisaama - Smile
Short Vowel: Kasra	Short Vowel: Ḍammah	Short Vowel: Fatḥa	Alif (أ) with Kasra sounds: 'I' — light & short, with a slight smile

Read & write from right to left

End	Middle	Beginning	Shape of Letter
ـا	ـا	أ	أ

آ

aa

Long Vowel: Alif

قُرْآن	آ	أو	إي
Quraan - The Quran	aa	oo	ee
Alif (أ) with long vowel Alif sounds: 'Aa' — light & long, with an open mouth	Long Vowel: Alif	Long Vowel: Waw	Long Vowel: Yaa

Read & write from right to left

End	Middle	Beginning	Shape of Letter
ـا	ـا	أ	أ

! Beginning or when preceded by a one-way connecter letter

أو

oo

Long Vowel: Waw

إي	أو	آ	أُولَاءِكَ
ee	oo	aa	oolaa-ika - Those
Long Vowel: Yaa	Long Vowel: Waw	Long Vowel: Alif	Alif (أ) with long vowel Waw sounds: 'Oo' — light & long, with a rounded mouth

Read & write from right to left

End	Middle	Beginning	Shape of Letter
ـا	ـا	أ	أ

إي

ee

Long Vowel: Yaa

إي	أو	آ	إيمان
ee	oo	aa	eeman - Faith" or "Belief
Long Vowel: Yaa	Long Vowel: Waw	Long Vowel: Alif	Alif (أ) with long vowel Yaa sounds: 'Ee' — light & long, with a wide smile

Read & write from right to left

End	Middle	Beginning	Shape of Letter
ـا	ـا	أ	أ

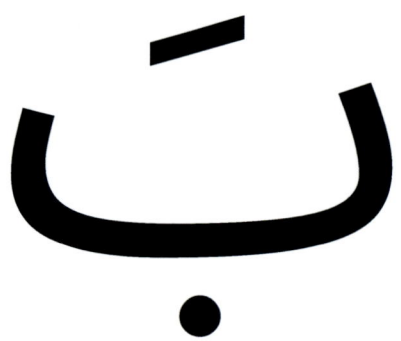

بَ

ba

Short Vowel: Fatḥa

بِ	بُ	بَ	بَقَرَة
bi	bo	ba	baqara - Cow
Short Vowel: Kasra	Short Vowel: Ḍammah	Short Vowel: Fatḥa	Baa (ب) with Fatḥa sounds: 'Ba' — light & short, with a slightly open mouth

Read & write from right to left

End	Middle	Beginning	Shape of Letter
ـب	ـبـ	بـ	ب

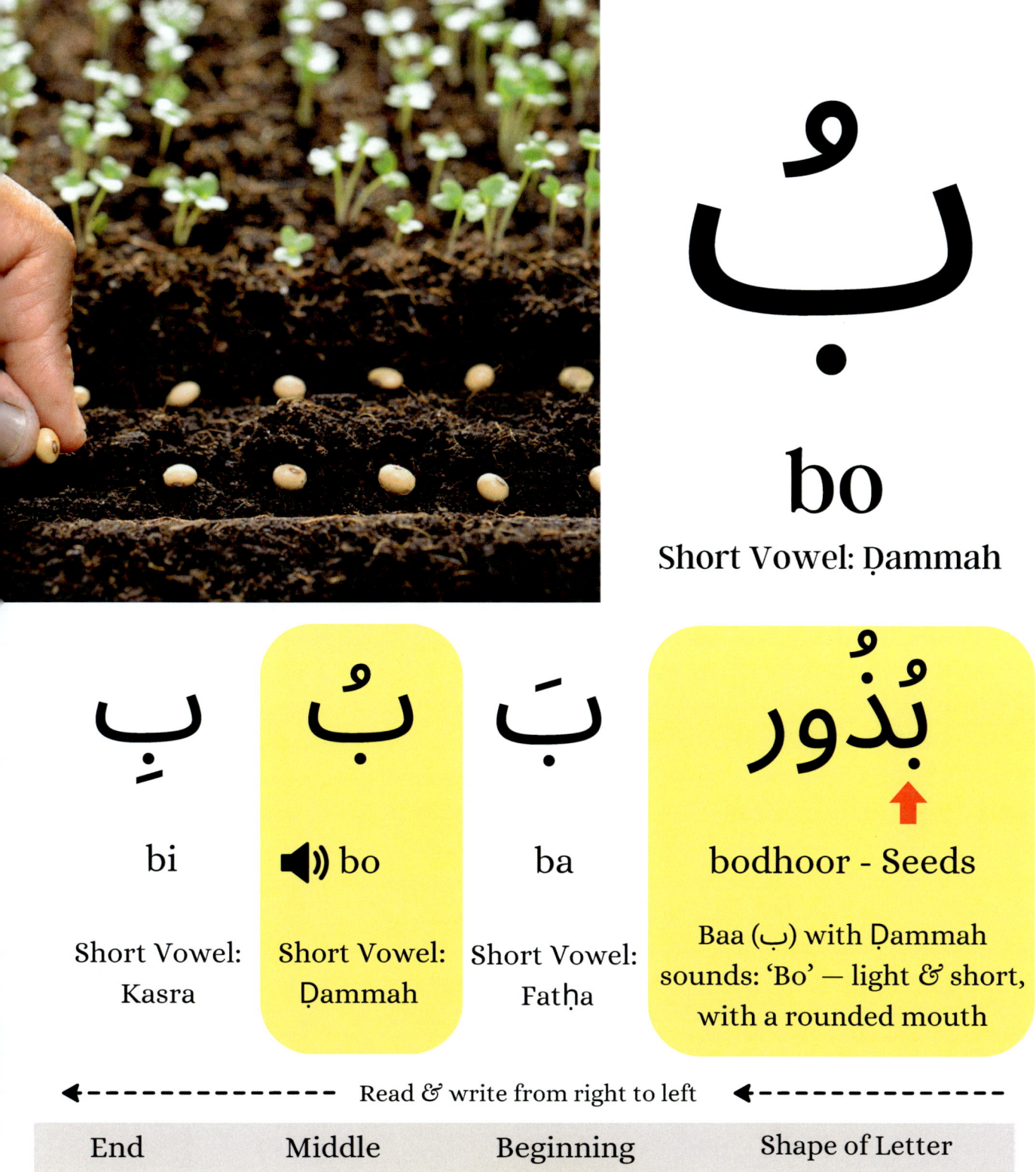

بُ

bo

Short Vowel: Ḍammah

بِ	بُ	بَ	بُذُور
bi	bo	ba	bodhoor - Seeds
Short Vowel: Kasra	Short Vowel: Ḍammah	Short Vowel: Fatḥa	Baa (ب) with Ḍammah sounds: 'Bo' — light & short, with a rounded mouth

Read & write from right to left

End	Middle	Beginning	Shape of Letter
ـب	ـبـ	بـ	ب

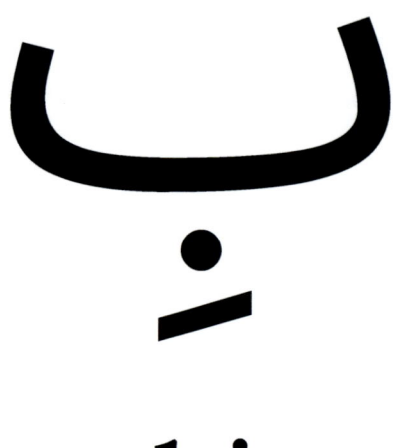

بِ

bi

Short Vowel: Kasra

بِ	بُ	بَ	بِسَاط
bi	bo	ba	bisaaṭ - Rug
Short Vowel: Kasra	Short Vowel: Ḍammah	Short Vowel: Fatḥa	Baa (ب) with Kasra sounds: 'Bi' — light & short, with a slight smile

Read & write from right to left

End	Middle	Beginning	Shape of Letter
ـب	ـبـ	بـ	ب

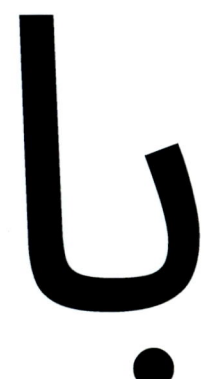

با

baa

Long Vowel: Alif

بي	بو	با	بَاب
bee	boo	baa	baab - Door
Long Vowel: Yaa	Long Vowel: Waw	Long Vowel: Alif	Baa (ب) with long vowel Alif sounds: 'Baa' — light & long, with an open mouth

Read & write from right to left

End	Middle	Beginning	Shape of Letter
ـب	ـبـ	بـ	ب

بو

boo

Long Vowel: Waw

بُوق	با	بو	بي
booq - Trumpet	baa	boo	bee
Baa (ب) with long vowel Waw sounds: 'Boo' — light & long, with a rounded mouth	Long Vowel: Alif	Long Vowel: Waw	Long Vowel: Yaa

Read & write from right to left

Shape of Letter	Beginning	Middle	End
ب	بـ	ـبـ	ـب

بي

bee

Long Vowel: Yaa

بي	بو	با	رَبِيع
bee	boo	baa	rabeeʿ - Spring
Long Vowel: Yaa	Long Vowel: Waw	Long Vowel: Alif	Baa (ب) with long vowel Yaa sounds: 'Bee' — light & long, with a wide smile

Read & write from right to left

End	Middle	Beginning	Shape of Letter
ـب	ـبـ	بـ	ب

Beginning: Beginning or when preceded by a one-way connecter letter

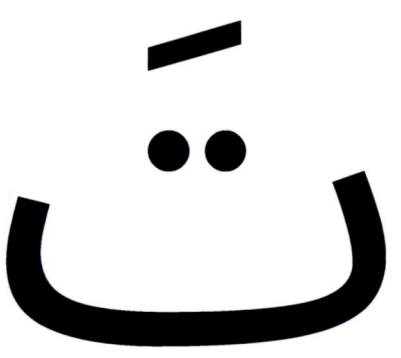

تَ

ta

Short Vowel: Fatḥa

تَصْوِير

taṣweer - Filming

Taa (ت) with Fatḥa sounds: 'Ta' — light & short, with a slightly open mouth

تِ	تُ	تَ
ti	to	ta
Short Vowel: Kasra	Short Vowel: Ḍammah	Short Vowel: Fatḥa

Read & write from right to left

End	Middle	Beginning	Shape of Letter
ـت	ـتـ	تـ	ت

تُ

to

Short Vowel: Ḍammah

تِ	تُ	تَ	تُفَّاحَة
ti	to	ta	toffaḥa - Apple
Short Vowel: Kasra	Short Vowel: Ḍammah	Short Vowel: Fatḥa	Taa (ت) with Ḍammah sounds: 'To' — light & short, with a rounded mouth

Read & write from right to left

End	Middle	Beginning	Shape of Letter
ـت	ـتـ	تـ	ت

تِ

ti

Short Vowel: Kasra

تِ	تُ	تَ	تِنِّين
ti	to	ta	tinneen - Dragon
Short Vowel: Kasra	Short Vowel: Ḍammah	Short Vowel: Fatḥa	Taa (ت) with Kasra sounds: 'Ti' — light & short, with a slight smile

Read & write from right to left

End	Middle	Beginning	Shape of Letter
ـت	ـتـ	تـ	ت

تا

taa

Long Vowel: Alif

تي	تو	تا	تَاج
tee	too	taa	taaj - Crown
Long Vowel: Yaa	Long Vowel: Waw	Long Vowel: Alif	Taa (ت) with long vowel Alif sounds: 'Taa' — light & long, with an open mouth

Read & write from right to left

End	Middle	Beginning	Shape of Letter
ـت	ـتـ	تـ	ت

تو

too

Long Vowel: Waw

تي	تو	تا	تُوت
tee	too	taa	toot - Mulberry
Long Vowel: Yaa	Long Vowel: Waw	Long Vowel: Alif	Taa (ت) with long vowel Waw sounds: 'Too' — light & long, with a rounded mouth

Read & write from right to left

End	Middle	Beginning	Shape of Letter
ـت	ـتـ	تـ	ت

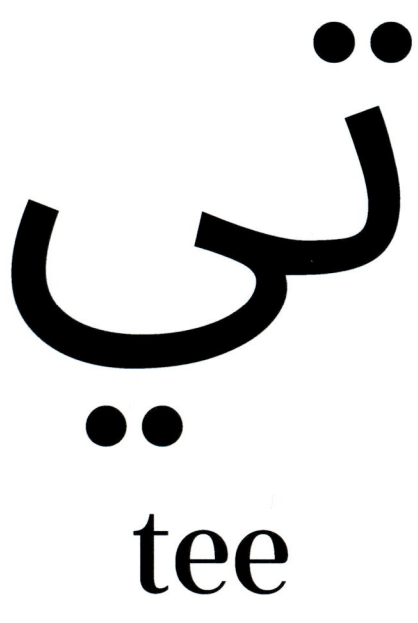

تي

tee

Long Vowel: Yaa

تي	تو	تا	تِين
tee	too	taa	teen - Fig
Long Vowel: Yaa	Long Vowel: Waw	Long Vowel: Alif	Taa (ت) with long vowel Yaa sounds: 'Tee' — light & long, with a wide smile

← - - - - - - - - - - - Read & write from right to left ← - - - - - - - - - - -

End	Middle	Beginning	Shape of Letter
ـت	ـتـ	تـ	ت

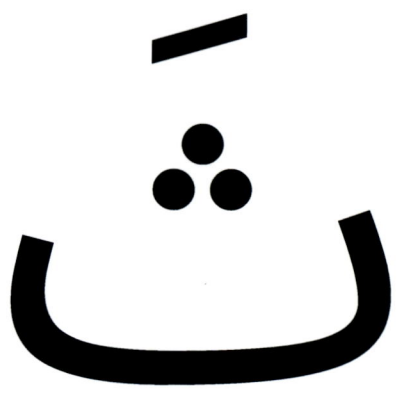

ثَ

tha

Short Vowel: Fatḥa

ثِ	ثُ	ثَ	ثَلْج
thi	tho	tha	thalj - Snow
Short Vowel: Kasra	Short Vowel: Ḍammah	Short Vowel: Fatḥa	Thaa (ث) with Fatḥa sounds: 'Tha' — light & short, with a slightly open mouth

Read & write from right to left

End	Middle	Beginning	Shape of Letter
ـث	ـثـ	ثـ	ث

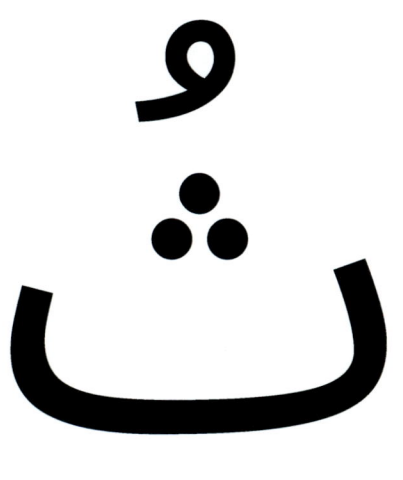

ثُ

tho

Short Vowel: Ḍammah

ثِ	ثُ	ثَ	ثُقْب
thi	tho	tha	thoqb - Hole
Short Vowel: Kasra	Short Vowel: Ḍammah	Short Vowel: Fatḥa	Thaa (ث) with Ḍammah sounds: 'Tho' — light & short, with a rounded mouth

Read & write from right to left

End	Middle	Beginning	Shape of Letter
ـث	ـثـ	ثـ	ث

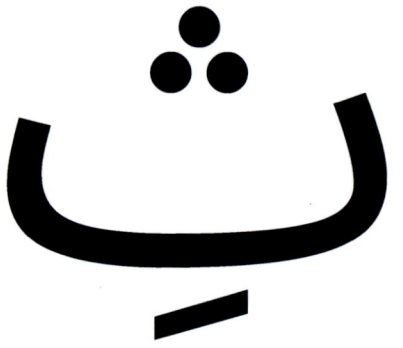

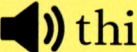

ثِ

thi

Short Vowel: Kasra

ثِ	ثُ	ثَ	ثِيَاب
thi	tho	tha	thiyaab - Clothes
Short Vowel: Kasra	Short Vowel: Ḍammah	Short Vowel: Fatḥa	Thaa (ث) with Kasra sounds: 'Thi' — light & short, with a slight smile

Read & write from right to left

End	Middle	Beginning	Shape of Letter
ـث	ـثـ	ثـ	ث

ثا

thaa

Long Vowel: Alif

ثي	ثو	ثا	ثَابِت
thee	thoo	thaa	thaabit - Steady
Long Vowel: Yaa	Long Vowel: Waw	Long Vowel: Alif	Thaa (ث) with long vowel Alif sounds: 'Thaa' — light & long, with an open mouth

Read & write from right to left

End	Middle	Beginning	Shape of Letter
ـث	ـثـ	ثـ	ث

ثو

thoo

Long Vowel: Waw

ثي	ثو	ثا	ثُوم
thee	thoo	thaa	thoom - Garlic
Long Vowel: Yaa	Long Vowel: Waw	Long Vowel: Alif	Thaa (ث) with long vowel Waw sounds: 'Thoo' — light & long, with a rounded mouth

Read & write from right to left

End	Middle	Beginning	Shape of Letter
ـث	ـثـ	ثـ	ث

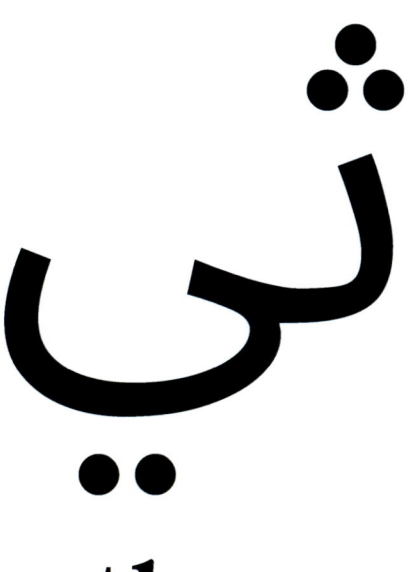

ثي

thee

Long Vowel: Yaa

ثي	ثو	ثا	مُثِير
thee	thoo	thaa	motheer - Thrilling
Long Vowel: Yaa	Long Vowel: Waw	Long Vowel: Alif	Thaa (ث) with long vowel Yaa sounds: 'Thee' — light & long, with a wide smile

Read & write from right to left

End	Middle	Beginning	Shape of Letter
ـث	ـثـ	ثـ	ث

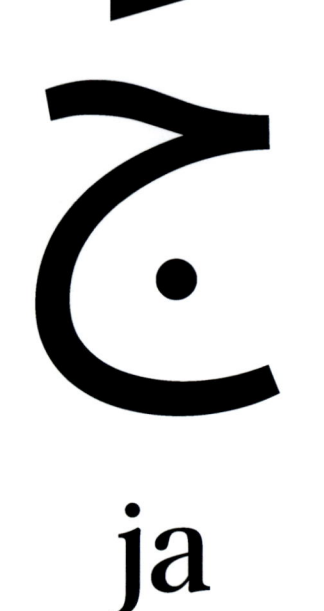

جَ

ja

Short Vowel: Fatḥa

جِ	جُ	جَ	جَمَل
ji	jo	ja	jamal - Camel
Short Vowel: Kasra	Short Vowel: Ḍammah	Short Vowel: Fatḥa	Jeem (ج) with Fatḥa sounds:'Ja' — light & short, with a slightly open mouth

Read & write from right to left

End	Middle	Beginning	Shape of Letter
ـج	ـجـ	جـ	ج

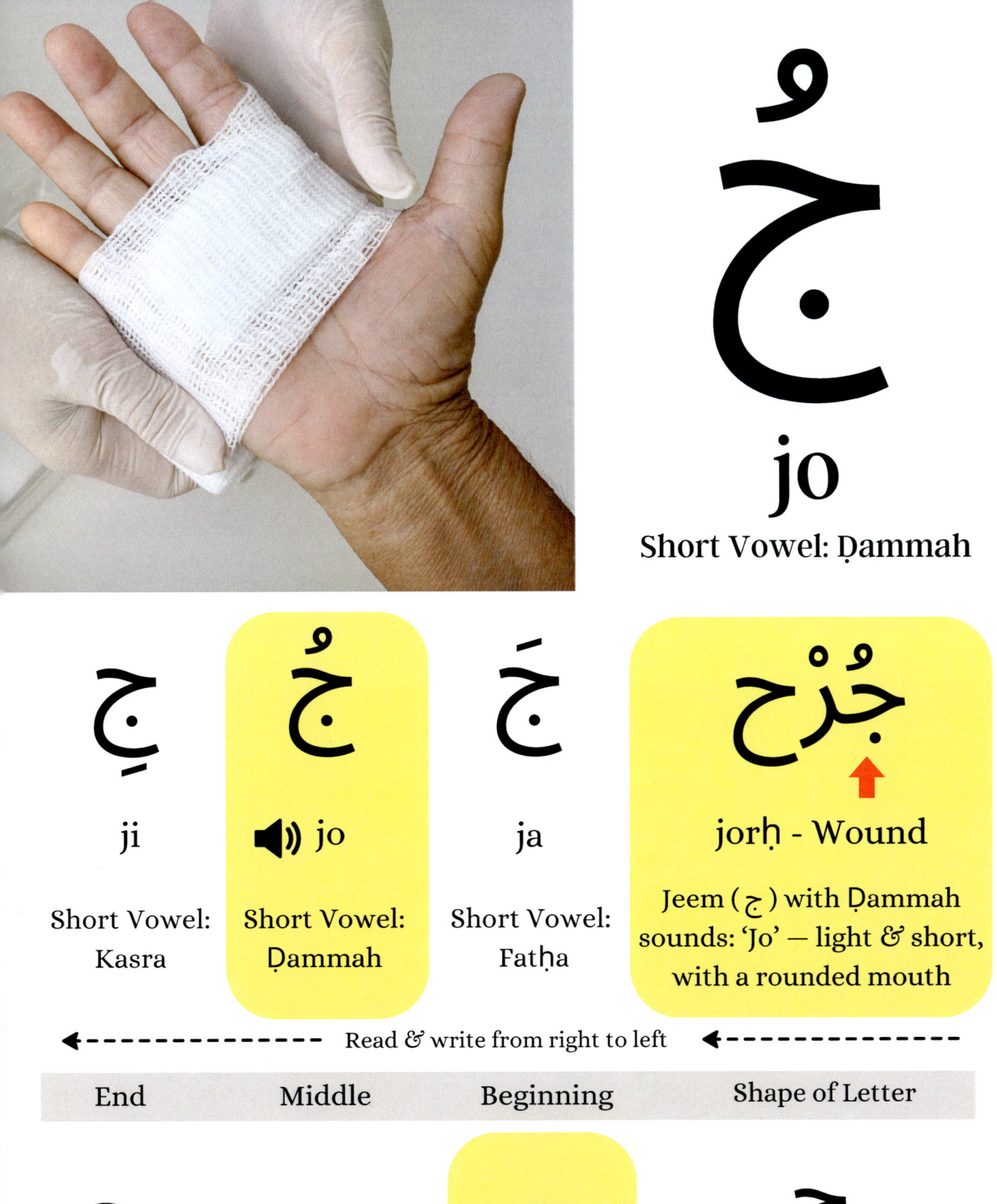

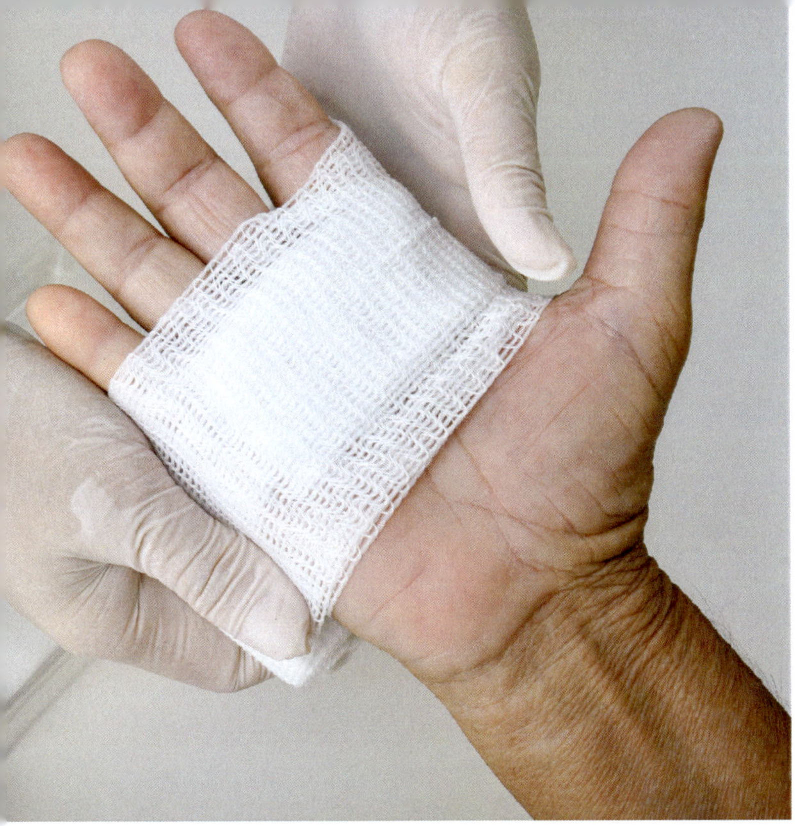

جُ

jo

Short Vowel: Ḍammah

جِ	جُ	جَ	جُرْح
ji	jo	ja	jorḥ - Wound
Short Vowel: Kasra	Short Vowel: Ḍammah	Short Vowel: Fatḥa	Jeem (ج) with Ḍammah sounds: 'Jo' — light & short, with a rounded mouth

Read & write from right to left

End	Middle	Beginning	Shape of Letter
ـج	ـجـ	جـ	ج

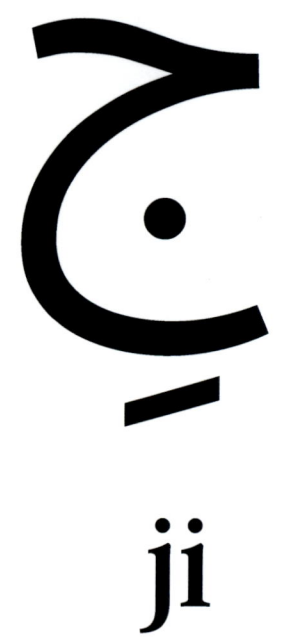

جِ

ji

Short Vowel: Kasra

جِ	جُ	جَ	جِبَال
ji	jo	ja	jibaal - Mountains
Short Vowel: Kasra	Short Vowel: Ḍammah	Short Vowel: Fatḥa	Jeem (ج) with Kasra sounds: 'Ji' — light & short, with a slight smile

Read & write from right to left

End	Middle	Beginning	Shape of Letter
ـج	ـجـ	جـ	ج

جا

jaa

Long Vowel: Alif

جي	جو	جا	حِجَارَة
jee	joo	jaa	ḥijaara - Stones
Long Vowel: Yaa	Long Vowel: Waw	Long Vowel: Alif	Jeem (ج) with long vowel Alif sounds: 'Jaa' — light & long, with an open mouth

Read & write from right to left

End	Middle	Beginning	Shape of Letter
ـج	ـجـ	جـ	ج

جُو

joo

Long Vowel: Waw

جِي	جُو	جَا	عَجُوز
jee	🔊 joo	jaa	ʿajooz - Elderly Woman
Long Vowel: Yaa	Long Vowel: Waw	Long Vowel: Alif	Jeem (ج) with long vowel Waw sounds: 'Joo' — light & long, with a rounded mouth

← - - - - - - - - - - - - - Read & write from right to left ← - - - - - - - - - - -

End	Middle	Beginning	Shape of Letter
ـج	ـجـ	جـ	ج

جي

jee

Long Vowel: Yaa

جي	جو	جا	جِيران
jee	joo	jaa	jeeran - Neighbors
Long Vowel: Yaa	Long Vowel: Waw	Long Vowel: Alif	Jeem (ج) with long vowel Yaa sounds: 'Jee' — light & long, with a wide smile

Read & write from right to left

End	Middle	Beginning	Shape of Letter
ـج	ـجـ	جـ	ج

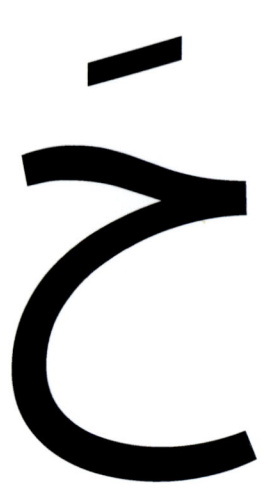

حَ

ḥa

Short Vowel: Fatḥa

حِ

ḥi

Short Vowel: Kasra

حُ

ḥo

Short Vowel: Ḍammah

حَ

ḥa

Short Vowel: Fatḥa

حَلِيب

ḥaleeb - Milk

Ḥaa (ح) with Fatḥa sounds: 'Ḥa' — deep, short, & throaty, like clearing the bottom of the throat, with a slightly open mouth (not in English)

Read & write from right to left

End	Middle	Beginning	Shape of Letter
ـح	ـحـ	حـ	ح

حُ

ḥo

Short Vowel: Ḍammah

حِ	حُ	حَ	حُبّ
ḥi	ḥo	ḥa	ḥobb - Love
Short Vowel: Kasra	Short Vowel: Ḍammah	Short Vowel: Fatḥa	Ḥaa (ح) with Ḍammah sounds: 'Ḥo' — deep, short, & throaty, like clearing the bottom of the throat, with a rounded mouth (not in English)

Read & write from right to left

End	Middle	Beginning	Shape of Letter
ـح	ـحـ	حـ	ح

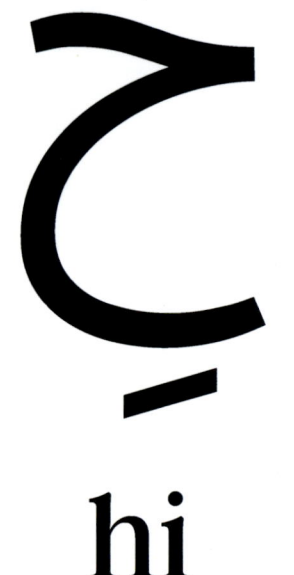

حِ

ḥi

Short Vowel: Kasra

حِ	حُ	حَ	حِمَار
ḥi	ḥo	ḥa	ḥimaar - Donkey
Short Vowel: Kasra	Short Vowel: Ḍammah	Short Vowel: Fatḥa	Ḥaa (ح) with Kasra sounds: 'Ḥi' — deep, short, & throaty, like clearing the bottom of the throat, with a slight smile (not in English)

Read & write from right to left

End	Middle	Beginning	Shape of Letter
ـح	ـحـ	حـ	ح

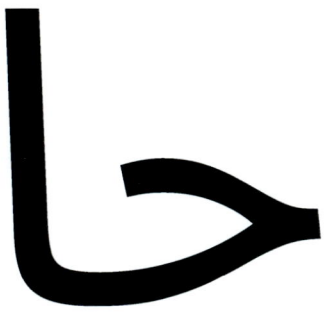

حا

ḥaa

Long Vowel: Alif

لَحَّام

laḥḥaam - Butcher

Ḥaa (ح) with long vowel Alif sounds: 'Ḥaa' — deep, throaty & long, like clearing the bottom of the throat, with an open mouth (not in English)

حي	حو	حا
ḥee	ḥoo	ḥaa
Long Vowel: Yaa	Long Vowel: Waw	Long Vowel: Alif

Read & write from right to left

End	Middle	Beginning	Shape of Letter
ـح	ـحـ	حـ	ح

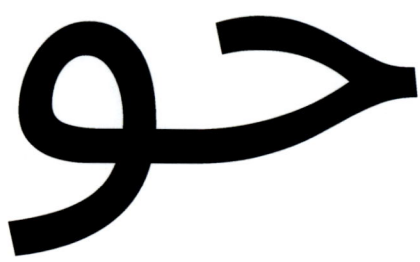

حو

ḥoo

Long Vowel: Waw

حي	حو	حا	حُوت
ḥee	ḥoo	ḥaa	ḥoot - Whale
Long Vowel: Yaa	Long Vowel: Waw	Long Vowel: Alif	Ḥaa (ح) with long vowel Waw sounds: 'Ḥoo' — deep, throaty & long, like clearing the bottom of the throat, with a rounded mouth (not in English)

Read & write from right to left

End	Middle	Beginning	Shape of Letter
ـح	ـحـ	حـ	ح

حي

ḥee

Long Vowel: Yaa

حي	حو	حا	مُحِيط
ḥee	ḥoo	ḥaa	moḥeeṭ - Ocean
Long Vowel: Yaa	Long Vowel: Waw	Long Vowel: Alif	Ḥaa (ح) with long vowel Yaa sounds: 'Ḥee' — deep, throaty & long, like clearing the bottom of the throat, with a wide smile (not in English)

Read & write from right to left

End	Middle	Beginning	Shape of Letter
ـح	ـحـ	حـ	ح

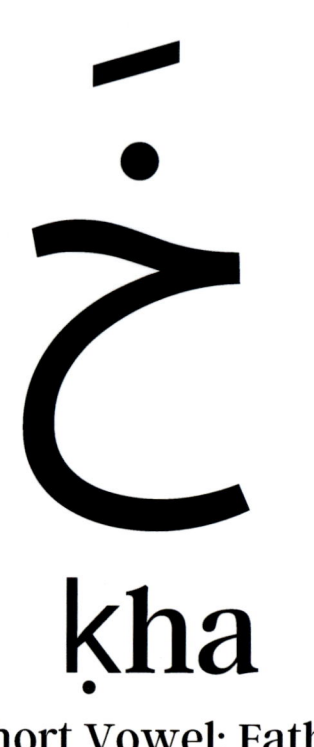

خَ

ḳha

Short Vowel: Fatḥa

خِ	خُ	خَ	خَرُوف
ḳhi	ḳho	ḳha	ḳharoof/Sheep
Short Vowel: Kasra	Short Vowel: Ḍammah	Short Vowel: Fatḥa	Ḳhaa (خ) with Fatḥa sounds: 'Ḳha' — deep, throaty & short, like clearing the top of the throat, with a slightly open mouth (not in English)

Read & write from right to left

End	Middle	Beginning	Shape of Letter
ـخ	ـخـ	خـ	خ

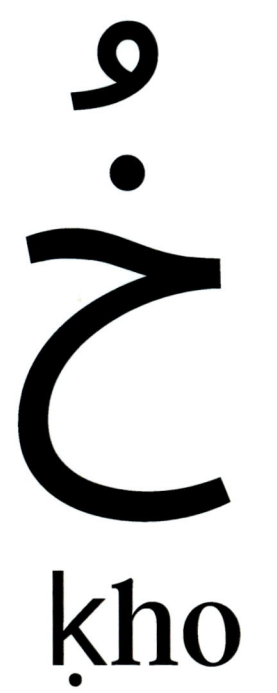

خُ

ḳho

Short Vowel: Ḍammah

خِ	خُ	خَ	خُبْز
ḳhi	ḳho	ḳha	ḳhobz - Bread
Short Vowel: Kasra	Short Vowel: Ḍammah	Short Vowel: Fatḥa	Ḳhaa (خ) with Ḍammah sounds: 'Ḳho' — deep, throaty & short, like clearing the top of the throat, with a rounded mouth (not in English)

Read & write from right to left

End	Middle	Beginning	Shape of Letter
ـخ	ـخـ	خـ	خ

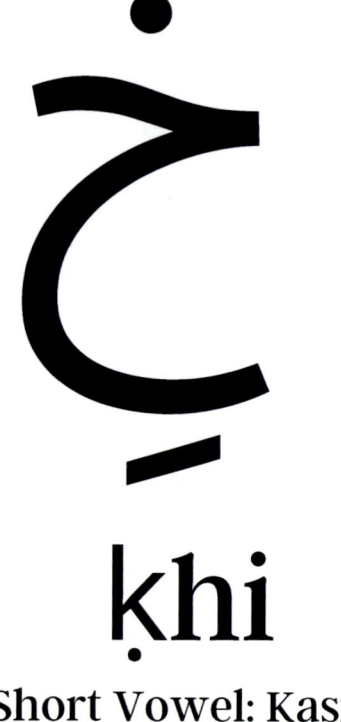

خِ

ḳhi

Short Vowel: Kasra

خِ	خُ	خَ	خِيَاطَة
ḳhi	ḳho	ḳha	ḳhiyaaṭa - Sewing
Short Vowel: Kasra	Short Vowel: Ḍammah	Short Vowel: Fatḥa	Ḳhaa (خ) with Kasra sounds: 'Ḳhi' — deep, throaty & short, like clearing the top of the throat, with a slight smile (not in English)

Read & write from right to left

End	Middle	Beginning	Shape of Letter
ـخ	ـخـ	خـ	خ

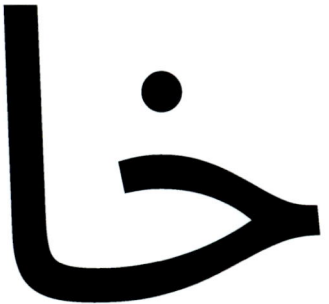

خا

ḳhaa

Long Vowel: Alif

خي	خو	خا	بُخَار
ḳhee	ḳhoo	ḳhaa	boḳhaar - Steam
Long Vowel: Yaa	Long Vowel: Waw	Long Vowel: Alif	Ḳhaa (خ) with long vowel Alif sounds: 'Ḳhaa' — deep, throaty & long, like clearing the top of the throat, with an open mouth (not in English)

Read & write from right to left

End	Middle	Beginning	Shape of Letter
ـخ	ـخـ	خـ	خ

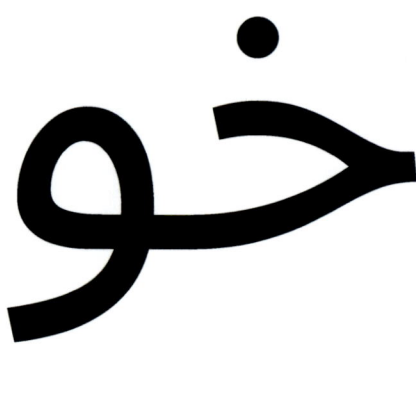

خو

ḳhoo

Long Vowel: Waw

خي	خو	خا	دُخُول
ḳhee	ḳhoo	ḳhaa	doḳhool - Entering
Long Vowel: Yaa	Long Vowel: Waw	Long Vowel: Alif	Ḳhaa (خ) with long vowel Waw sounds: 'Ḳhoo' — deep, throaty & long, like clearing the top of the throat, with a rounded mouth (not in English)

Read & write from right to left

End	Middle	Beginning	Shape of Letter
ـخ	ـخـ	خـ	خ

! Beginning or when preceded by a one-way connecter letter

خي

ḳhee

Long Vowel: Yaa

مُخِيف

moḳheef - Scary

Ḳhaa (خ) with long vowel Yaa sounds: 'Ḳhee' — deep, throaty & long, like clearing the top of the throat, with a wide smile (not in English)

خا	خو	خي
ḳhaa	ḳhoo	ḳhee
Long Vowel: Alif	Long Vowel: Waw	Long Vowel: Yaa

Read & write from right to left

Shape of Letter	Beginning	Middle	End
خ	خـ	ـخـ	ـخ

دَ

da

Short Vowel: Fatḥa

دِ	دُ	دَ	دَجَاجَة
di	do	da	dajaaja - Chicken
Short Vowel: Kasra	Short Vowel: Ḍammah	Short Vowel: Fatḥa	Daal (د) with Fatḥa sounds: 'Da' — light & short, with a slightly open mouth

Read & write from right to left

End	Middle	Beginning	Shape of Letter
ـد	ـد	د	د

دُ

do

Short Vowel: Ḍammah

دِ	دُ	دَ	دُبّ
di	do	da	dobb - Bear
Short Vowel: Kasra	Short Vowel: Ḍammah	Short Vowel: Fatḥa	Daal (د) with Ḍammah sounds: 'Do' — light & short, with a rounded mouth

Read & write from right to left

End	Middle	Beginning	Shape of Letter
ـد	ـد	د	د

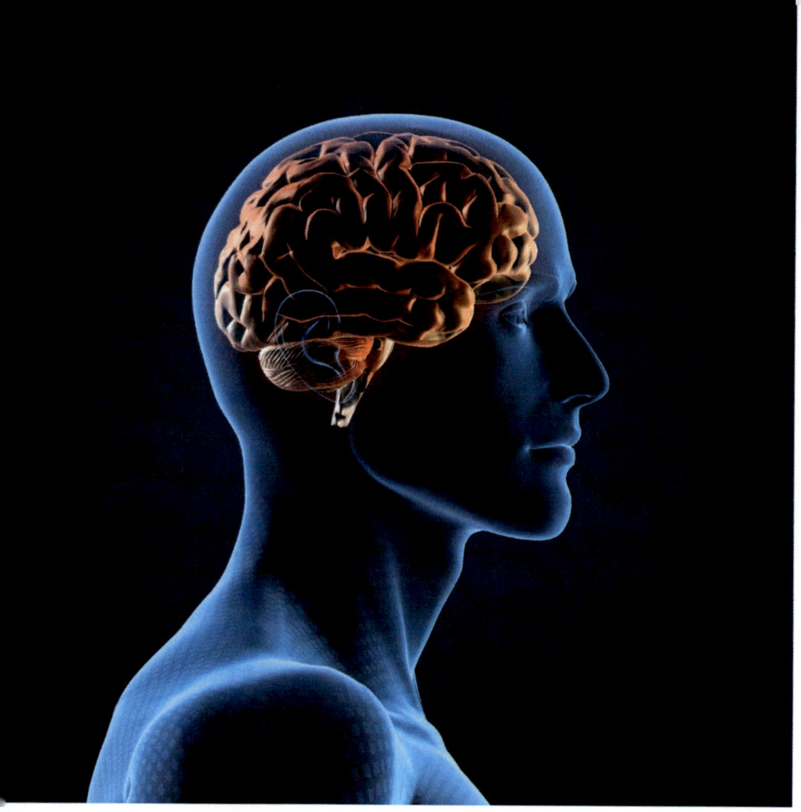

دِ

di

Short Vowel: Kasra

دِ	دُ	دَ	دِمَاغ
di	do	da	dimaagh - Brain
Short Vowel: Kasra	Short Vowel: Ḍammah	Short Vowel: Fatḥa	Daal (د) with Kasra sounds: 'Di' — light & short, with a slight smile

Read & write from right to left

End	Middle	Beginning	Shape of Letter
ـد	ـد	د	د

دا

daa

Long Vowel: Alif

دي	دو	دا	دَار
dee	doo	daa	daar - House
Long Vowel: Yaa	Long Vowel: Waw	Long Vowel: Alif	Daal (د) with long vowel Alif sounds: 'Daa' — light & long, with an open mouth

Read & write from right to left

End	Middle	Beginning	Shape of Letter
ـد	ـد	د	د

دو

doo

Long Vowel: Waw

دي	دو	دا	دُود
dee	doo	daa	dood- Worms
Long Vowel: Yaa	Long Vowel: Waw	Long Vowel: Alif	Daal (د) with long vowel Waw sounds: 'Doo' — light & long, with a rounded mouth

Read & write from right to left

End	Middle	Beginning	Shape of Letter
ـد	ـد	د	د

دي

dee

Long Vowel: Yaa

دي	دو	دا	دِيك
dee	doo	daa	deek - Rooster
Long Vowel: Yaa	Long Vowel: Waw	Long Vowel: Alif	Daal (د) with long vowel Yaa sounds: 'Dee' — light & long, with a wide smile

Read & write from right to left

End	Middle	Beginning	Shape of Letter
ـد	ـد	د	د

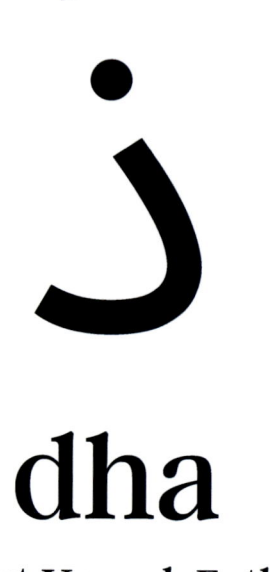

ذَ

dha

Short Vowel: Fatḥa

ذِ	ذُ	ذَ	ذَنَب
dhi	dho	dha	dhanab - Tail
Short Vowel: Kasra	Short Vowel: Ḍammah	Short Vowel: Fatḥa	Dhaal (ذ) with Fatḥa sounds: 'Dha' — light & short, with a slightly open mouth

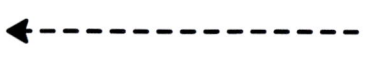

Read & write from right to left

End	Middle	Beginning	Shape of Letter
ـذ	ـذ	ذ	ذ

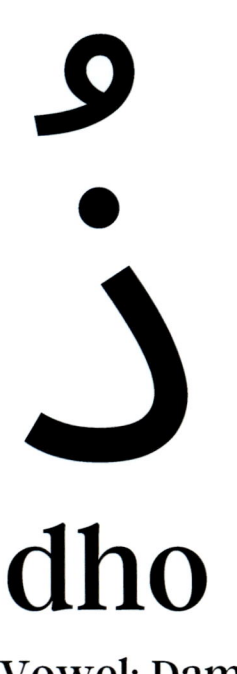

ذُ

dho

Short Vowel: Ḍammah

ذِ	ذُ	ذَ	ذُرَة
dhi	dho	dha	dhora - Corn
Short Vowel: Kasra	Short Vowel: Ḍammah	Short Vowel: Fatḥa	Dhaal (ذ) with Ḍammah sounds: 'Dho' — light & short, with a rounded mouth

Read & write from right to left

End	Middle	Beginning	Shape of Letter
ـذ	ـذ	ذ	ذ

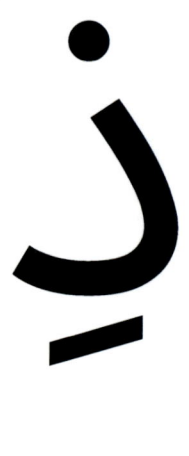

ذِ

dhi

Short Vowel: Kasra

ذِئْب

dhib - Wolf

Dhaal (ذ) with Kasra sounds: ‘Dhi’ — light & short, with a slight smile

ذَ

dha

Short Vowel: Fatḥa

ذُ

dho

Short Vowel: Ḍammah

ذِ

dhi

Short Vowel: Kasra

Read & write from right to left

End	Middle	Beginning	Shape of Letter
ـذ	ـذ	ذ	ذ

ذا

dhaa

Long Vowel: Alif

ذي	ذو	ذا	رَذَاذ
dhee	dhoo	dhaa	radhaadh - Mist
Long Vowel: Yaa	Long Vowel: Waw	Long Vowel: Alif	Dhaal (ذ) with long vowel Alif sounds: 'Dhaa' — light & long, with an open mouth

Read & write from right to left

End	Middle	Beginning	Shape of Letter
ـذ	ـذ	ذ	ذ

Beginning or when preceded by a one-way connecter letter

ذو

dhoo

Long Vowel: Waw

ذي	ذو	ذا	جُذُور
dhee	dhoo	dhaa	jodhoor - Roots
Long Vowel: Yaa	Long Vowel: Waw	Long Vowel: Alif	Dhaal (ذ) with long vowel Waw sounds: 'Dhoo' — light & long, with a rounded mouth

Read & write from right to left

End	Middle	Beginning	Shape of Letter
ـذ	ـذ	ذ	ذ

ذي

dhee

Long Vowel: Yaa

ذي	ذو	ذا	مُذِيع
dhee	dhoo	dhaa	modheeʿ - Broadcaster
Long Vowel: Yaa	Long Vowel: Waw	Long Vowel: Alif	Dhaal (ذ) with long vowel Yaa sounds: 'Dhee' — light & long, with a wide smile

Read & write from right to left

End	Middle	Beginning	Shape of Letter
ـذ	ـذ	ذ	ذ

رَ

ra

Short Vowel: Fatḥa

رِ	رُ	رَ	رَجُل
ri	ro	ra	rajol - Man
Short Vowel: Kasra	Short Vowel: Ḍammah	Short Vowel: Fatḥa	Raa (ر) with Fatḥa sounds: 'Ra' — light & short, with a slightly open mouth

Read & write from right to left

End	Middle	Beginning	Shape of Letter
ـر	ـر	ر	ر

رُ

ro

Short Vowel: Ḍammah

رِ	رُ	رَ	رُمَّان
ri	ro	ra	romman - Pomegranate
Short Vowel: Kasra	Short Vowel: Ḍammah	Short Vowel: Fatḥa	Raa (ر) with Ḍammah sounds: 'Ro' — light & short, with a rounded mouth

Read & write from right to left

End	Middle	Beginning	Shape of Letter
ـر	ـر	ر	ر

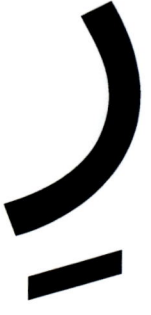

رِ

ri

Short Vowel: Kasra

رِ	رُ	رَ	رِيَاح
ri	ro	ra	riyaaḥ - Wind
Short Vowel: Kasra	Short Vowel: Ḍammah	Short Vowel: Fatḥa	Raa (ر) with Kasra sounds: 'Ri' — light & short, with a slight smile

Read & write from right to left

End	Middle	Beginning	Shape of Letter
ـر	ـر	ر	ر

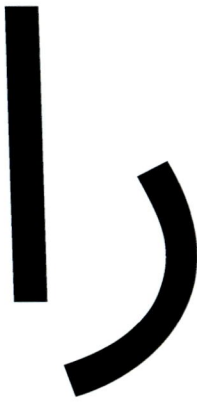

را

raa

Long Vowel: Alif

ري	رو	را	رَاكُون
ree	roo	raa	raakoon - Raccoon
Long Vowel: Yaa	Long Vowel: Waw	Long Vowel: Alif	Raa (ر) with long vowel Alif sounds: 'Raa' — light & long, with an open mouth

Read & write from right to left

End	Middle	Beginning	Shape of Letter
ـر	ـر	ر	ر

رو

roo

Long Vowel: Waw

ري	رو	را	مُرُوج
ree	roo	raa	morooj - Meadow
Long Vowel: Yaa	Long Vowel: Waw	Long Vowel: Alif	Raa (ر) with long vowel Waw sounds: 'Roo' — light & long, with a rounded mouth

Read & write from right to left

End	Middle	Beginning	Shape of Letter
ـر	ـر	ر	ر

ري

ree

Long Vowel: Yaa

ري	رو	را	خَرِيف
ree	roo	raa	ḳhareef - Autumn
Long Vowel: Yaa	Long Vowel: Waw	Long Vowel: Alif	Raa (ر) with long vowel Yaa sounds: 'Ree' — light & long, with a wide smile

Read & write from right to left

End	Middle	Beginning	Shape of Letter
ـر	ـر	ر	ر

زَ

za

Short Vowel: Fatḥa

زِ	زُ	زَ	زَرَافَة
zi	zo	za	zarafah - Giraffe
Short Vowel: Kasra	Short Vowel: Ḍammah	Short Vowel: Fatḥa	Zay (ز) with Fatḥa sounds: 'Za' — light & short, with a slightly open mouth

Read & write from right to left

End	Middle	Beginning	Shape of Letter
ـز	ـز	ز	ز

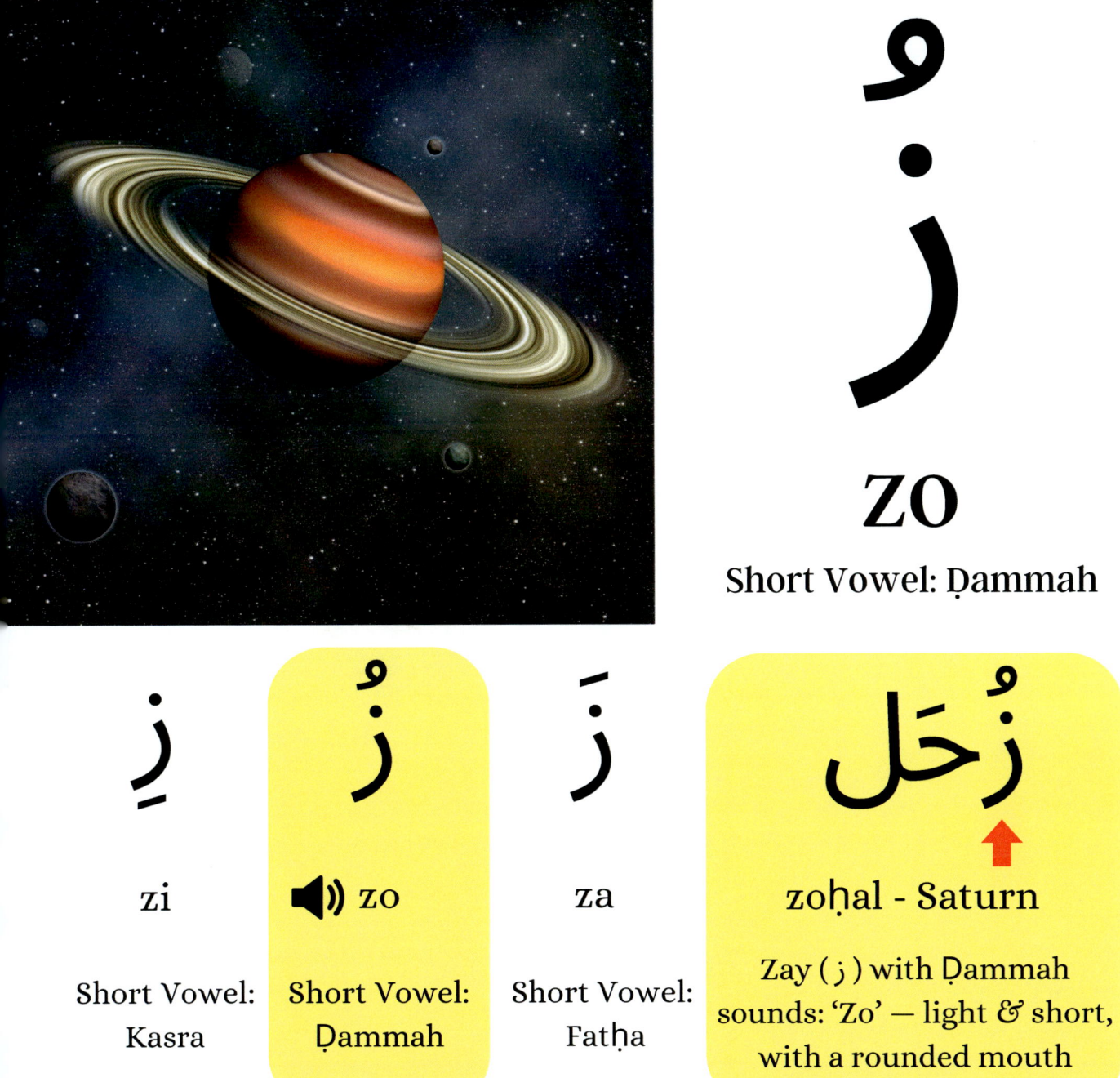

زُ

ZO

Short Vowel: Ḍammah

زِ	زُ	زَ	زُحَل
zi	zo	za	zoḥal - Saturn
Short Vowel: Kasra	Short Vowel: Ḍammah	Short Vowel: Fatḥa	Zay (ز) with Ḍammah sounds: 'Zo' — light & short, with a rounded mouth

Read & write from right to left

End	Middle	Beginning	Shape of Letter
ـز	ـز	ز	ز

زِ

Zi

Short Vowel: Kasra

زِ	زُ	زَ	زِرَاعَة
zi	zo	za	ziraaʿa – Planting
Short Vowel: Kasra	Short Vowel: Ḍammah	Short Vowel: Fatḥa	Zay (ز) with Kasra sounds: 'Zi' — light & short, with a slight smile

Read & write from right to left

End	Middle	Beginning	Shape of Letter
ـز	ـز	ز	ز

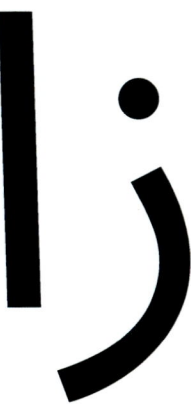

زا

zaa

Long Vowel: Alif

زي	زو	زا	مِيزَان
zee	zoo	zaa	meezaan - Scale
Long Vowel: Yaa	Long Vowel: Waw	Long Vowel: Alif	Zay (ز) with long vowel Alif sounds: 'Zaa' – light & long, with an open mouth

Read & write from right to left

End	Middle	Beginning	Shape of Letter
ـز	ـزـ	ز	ز

زو

ZOO

Long Vowel: Waw

زي	زو	زا	تَزُور
zee	zoo	zaa	tazoor - To Visit
Long Vowel: Yaa	Long Vowel: Waw	Long Vowel: Alif	Zay (ز) with long vowel Waw sounds: 'Zoo' — light & long, with a rounded mouth

Read & write from right to left

End	Middle	Beginning	Shape of Letter
ـز	ـز	ز	ز

زي

zee

Long Vowel: Yaa

زي	زو	زا	جَزِيرَة
zee	zoo	zaa	jazeerah - Island
Long Vowel: Yaa	Long Vowel: Waw	Long Vowel: Alif	Zay (ز) with long vowel Yaa sounds: 'Zee' — light & long, with a wide smile

Read & write from right to left

End	Middle	Beginning	Shape of Letter
ـز	ـز	ز	ز

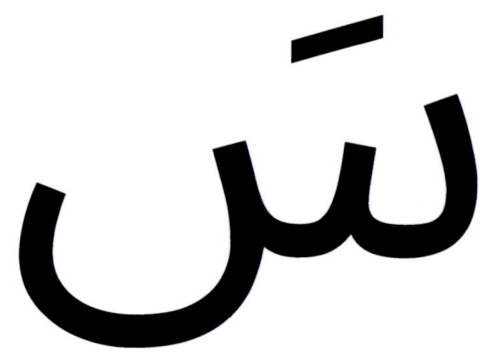

سَ

sa

Short Vowel: Fatḥa

بِس	سُ	سَ	سَمَك
si	so	sa	samak - Fish
Short Vowel: Kasra	Short Vowel: Ḍammah	Short Vowel: Fatḥa	Seen (س) with Fatḥa sounds: 'Sa' — light & short, with a slightly open mouth

Read & write from right to left

End	Middle	Beginning	Shape of Letter
ـس	ـسـ	سـ	س

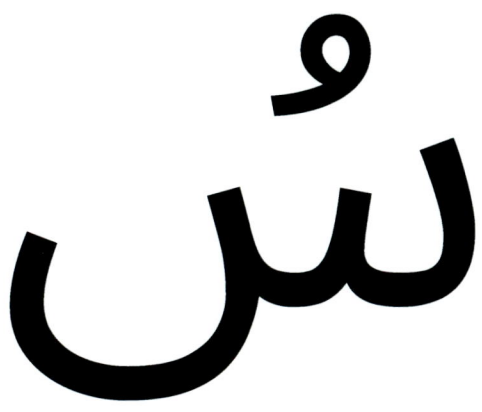

سُ

so

Short Vowel: Ḍammah

سِ	سُ	سَ	سُكَّر
si	so	sa	sokkar - Sugar
Short Vowel: Kasra	Short Vowel: Ḍammah	Short Vowel: Fatḥa	Seen (س) with Ḍammah sounds: 'So' — light & short, with a rounded mouth

Read & write from right to left

End	Middle	Beginning	Shape of Letter
ـس	ـسـ	سـ	س

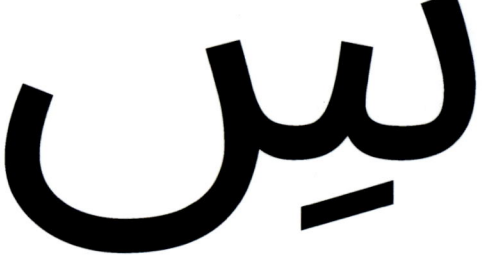

سِ

Si

Short Vowel: Kasra

سِ	سُ	سَ	سِبَاحَةٌ
si	so	sa	sibaaḥa - Swimming
Short Vowel: Kasra	Short Vowel: Ḍammah	Short Vowel: Fatḥa	Seen (س) with Kasra sounds: 'Si' — light & short, with a slight smile

Read & write from right to left

End	Middle	Beginning	Shape of Letter
ـس	ـسـ	سـ	س

سا

saa

Long Vowel: Alif

سـي	سـو	سا	سَاعَة
see	soo	saa	saaʿa – Watch
Long Vowel: Yaa	Long Vowel: Waw	Long Vowel: Alif	Seen (س) with long vowel Alif sounds: 'Saa' — light & long, with an open mouth

Read & write from right to left

End	Middle	Beginning	Shape of Letter
ـس	ـسـ	سـ	س

سو

soo

Long Vowel: Waw

سي	سو	سا	سُوق
see	soo	saa	sooq - Market
Long Vowel: Yaa	Long Vowel: Waw	Long Vowel: Alif	Seen (س) with long vowel Waw sounds: 'Soo' — light & long, with a rounded mouth

Read & write from right to left

End	Middle	Beginning	Shape of Letter
ـس	ـسـ	سـ	س

سِي

see

Long Vowel: Yaa

سِي	سُو	سَا	سِينَمَا
see	soo	saa	seenama - Cinema
Long Vowel: Yaa	Long Vowel: Waw	Long Vowel: Alif	Seen (س) with long vowel Yaa sounds: 'See' — light & long, with a wide smile

Read & write from right to left

End	Middle	Beginning	Shape of Letter
ـس	ـسـ	سـ	س

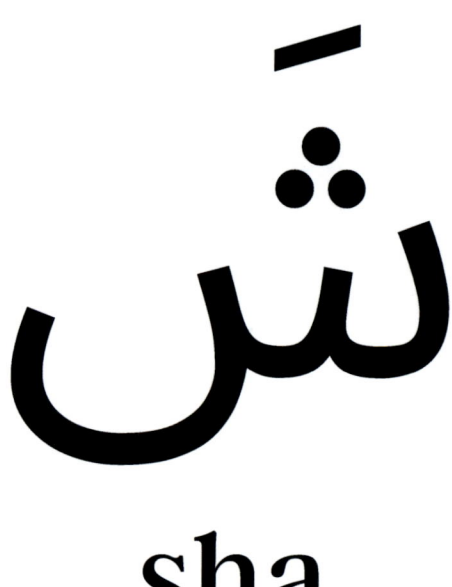

شَ

sha

Short Vowel: Fatḥa

شِ	شُ	شَ	شَمس
shi	sho	sha	shams - Sun
Short Vowel: Kasra	Short Vowel: Ḍammah	Short Vowel: Fatḥa	Sheen (ش) with Fatḥa sounds: 'Sha' — light & short, with a slightly open mouth

Read & write from right to left

End	Middle	Beginning	Shape of Letter
ـش	ـشـ	شـ	ش

شُ

sho

Short Vowel: Ḍammah

شُمَّام	شَ	شُ	شِ
shommaam - Cantaloupe	sha	sho	shi
Sheen (ش) with Ḍammah sounds: 'Sho' – light & short, with a rounded mouth	Short Vowel: Fatḥa	Short Vowel: Ḍammah	Short Vowel: Kasra

Read & write from right to left

Shape of Letter	Beginning	Middle	End
ش	شـ	ـشـ	ـش

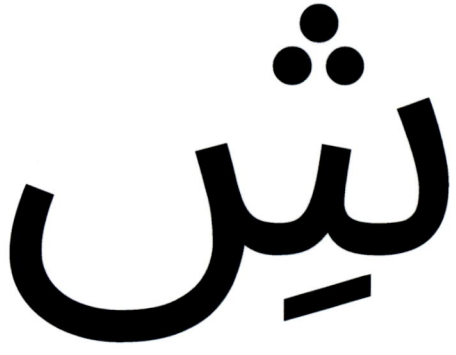

شِ

shi

Short Vowel: Kasra

شِ	شُ	شَ	شِرَاع
shi	sho	sha	shiraaʿ – Sail
Short Vowel: Kasra	Short Vowel: Ḍammah	Short Vowel: Fatḥa	Sheen (ش) with Kasra sounds: 'Shi' — light & short, with a slight smile

Read & write from right to left

End	Middle	Beginning	Shape of Letter
ـش	ـشـ	شـ	ش

شا

shaa

Long Vowel: Alif

شَارِع

shaari' - Street

Sheen (ش) with long vowel Alif sounds: 'Shaa' — light & long, with an open mouth

شا

shaa

Long Vowel: Alif

شو

shoo

Long Vowel: Waw

شي

shee

Long Vowel: Yaa

Read & write from right to left

Shape of Letter	Beginning	Middle	End
ش	شـ	ـشـ	ـش

شو

shoo

Long Vowel: Waw

شي	شو	شا	قُشُور
shee	shoo	shaa	qoshoor - Peels
Long Vowel: Yaa	Long Vowel: Waw	Long Vowel: Alif	Sheen (ش) with long vowel Waw sounds: 'Shoo' — light & long, with a rounded mouth

← - - - - - - - - - - - - - - Read & write from right to left ← - - - - - - - - - - - - - -

End	Middle	Beginning	Shape of Letter
ـش	ـشـ	شـ	ش

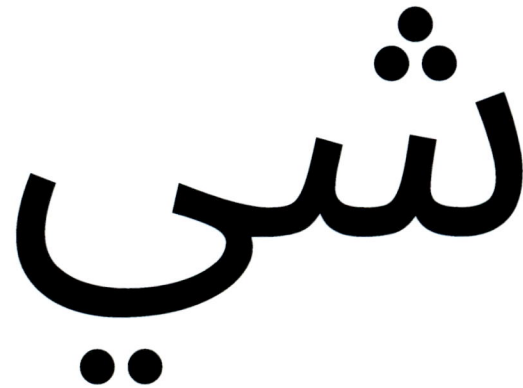

شي

shee

Long Vowel: Yaa

شي	شو	شا	حَشِيش
shee	shoo	shaa	ḥasheesh - Grass
Long Vowel: Yaa	Long Vowel: Waw	Long Vowel: Alif	Sheen (ش) with long vowel Yaa sounds: 'Shee' — light & long, with a wide smile

Read & write from right to left

End	Middle	Beginning	Shape of Letter
ـش	ـشـ	شـ	ش

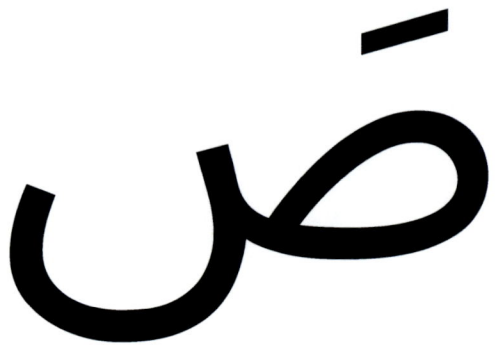

صَ

ṣa

Short Vowel: Fatḥa

صِ	صُ	صَ	صَحْنٌ
ṣi	ṣo	ṣa	ṣaḥn - Plate
Short Vowel: Kasra	Short Vowel: Ḍammah	Short Vowel: Fatḥa	Ṣaad (ص) with Fatḥa sounds: 'Ṣa' — deep & short, with a slightly open mouth

← - - - - - - - - - - - - Read & write from right to left ← - - - - - - - - - - - -

End	Middle	Beginning	Shape of Letter
ـص	ـصـ	صـ	ص

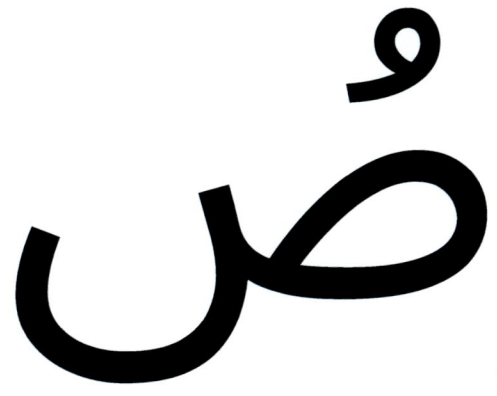

صُ

Ṣo

Short Vowel: Ḍammah

صِ	صُ	صَ	صُخُور
ṣi	ṣo	ṣa	ṣoḳhoor - Rocks
Short Vowel: Kasra	Short Vowel: Ḍammah	Short Vowel: Fatḥa	Ṣaad (ص) with Ḍammah sounds: 'Ṣo' — deep & short, with a rounded mouth

Read & write from right to left

End	Middle	Beginning	Shape of Letter
ـص	ـصـ	صـ	ص

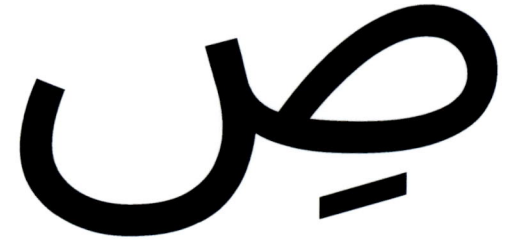

صِ

Ṣi

Short Vowel: Kasra

صِ	صُ	صَ	صِيَاح
Ṣi	Ṣo	Ṣa	Ṣiyaaḥ - Shouting
Short Vowel: Kasra	Short Vowel: Ḍammah	Short Vowel: Fatḥa	Ṣaad (ص) with Kasra sounds: 'Ṣi' — deep & short, with a slight smile

Read & write from right to left

End	Middle	Beginning	Shape of Letter
ـص	ـصـ	صـ	ص

صا

Ṣaa

Long Vowel: Alif

صي	صو	صا	صَابُون
Ṣee	Ṣoo	Ṣaa	Ṣaaboon - Soap
Long Vowel: Yaa	Long Vowel: Waw	Long Vowel: Alif	Ṣaad (ص) with long vowel Alif sounds: 'Ṣaa' — deep & long, with an open mouth

Read & write from right to left

End	Middle	Beginning	Shape of Letter
ـص	ـصـ	صـ	ص

صو

Ṣoo

Long Vowel: Waw

صي	صو	صا	صُوص
Ṣee	Ṣoo	Ṣaa	Ṣooṣ - Chick
Long Vowel: Yaa	Long Vowel: Waw	Long Vowel: Alif	Ṣaad (ص) with long vowel Waw sounds: 'Ṣoo' — deep & long, with a rounded mouth

Read & write from right to left

End	Middle	Beginning	Shape of Letter
ـص	ـصـ	صـ	ص

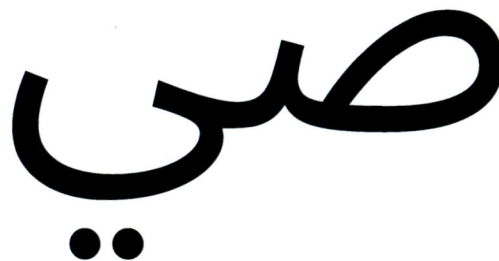

صي

ṣee

Long Vowel: Yaa

صي	صو	صا	عَصِير
ṣee	ṣoo	ṣaa	ʿaṣeer - Juice
Long Vowel: Yaa	Long Vowel: Waw	Long Vowel: Alif	Ṣaad (ص) with long vowel Yaa sounds: 'Ṣee' — deep & long, with a wide smile

Read & write from right to left

End	Middle	Beginning	Shape of Letter
ـص	ـصـ	صـ	ص

ضَ

ḍa

Short Vowel: Fatḥa

ضِ ضُ ضَ ضَحِك

ḍi ḍo ḍa ḍaḥik - Laughter

Short Vowel: Kasra

Short Vowel: Ḍammah

Short Vowel: Fatḥa

Ḍaad (ض) with Fatḥa sounds: 'Ḍa' — deep & short, with a slightly open mouth

Read & write from right to left

End	Middle	Beginning	Shape of Letter
ـض	ـضـ	ضـ	ض

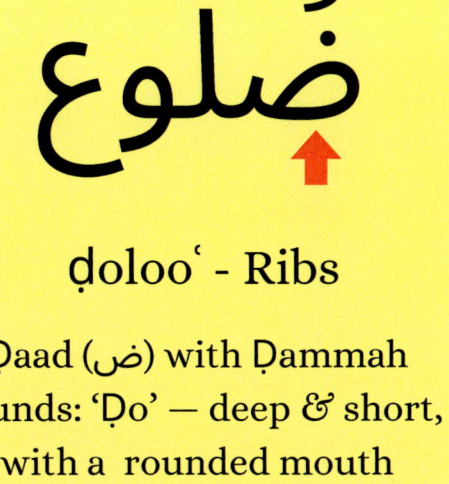

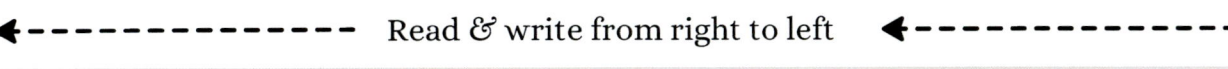

ضُ

ḍo

Short Vowel: Ḍammah

ضِ	ضُ	ضَ	ضُلُوع
ḍi	ḍo	ḍa	ḍoloo' - Ribs
Short Vowel: Kasra	Short Vowel: Ḍammah	Short Vowel: Fatḥa	Ḍaad (ض) with Ḍammah sounds: 'Ḍo' — deep & short, with a rounded mouth

Read & write from right to left

End	Middle	Beginning	Shape of Letter
ـض	ـضـ	ضـ	ض

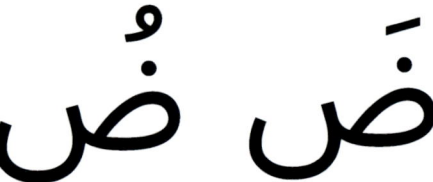

ضِ

ḍi

Short Vowel: Kasra

ضِ	ضُ	ضَ	ضِفْدَع
ḍi	ḍo	ḍa	ḍifdaʿ - Frog
Short Vowel: Kasra	Short Vowel: Ḍammah	Short Vowel: Fatḥa	Ḍaad (ض) with Kasra sounds: 'Ḍi' — deep & short, with a slight smile

Read & write from right to left

End	Middle	Beginning	Shape of Letter
ـض	ـضـ	ضـ	ض

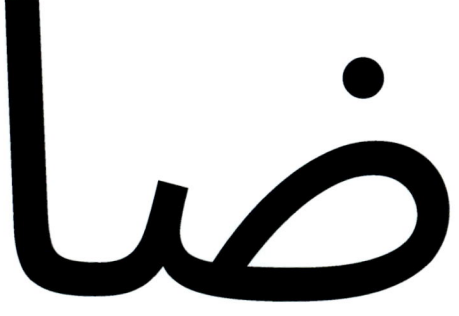

ضا

ḍaa

Long Vowel: Alif

ضَابِط	ضا	ضو	ضي
ḍaabiṭ - Officer	ḍaa	ḍoo	ḍee
Ḍaad (ض) with long vowel Alif sounds: 'Ḍaa' — deep & long, with an open mouth	Long Vowel: Alif	Long Vowel: Waw	Long Vowel: Yaa

Read & write from right to left

Shape of Letter	Beginning	Middle	End
ض	ضـ	ـضـ	ـض

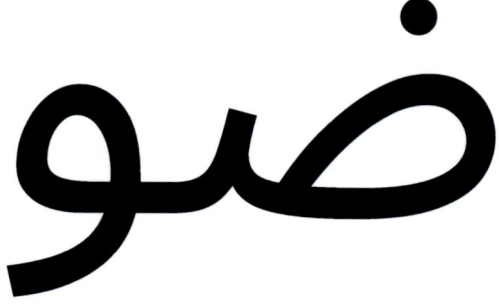

ضو

ḍoo

Long Vowel: Waw

ضي	ضو	ضا	فُضُول
ḍee	ḍoo	ḍaa	foḍool - Curiosity
Long Vowel: Yaa	Long Vowel: Waw	Long Vowel: Alif	Ḍaad (ض) with long vowel Waw sounds: 'Ḍoo' — deep & long, with a rounded mouth

Read & write from right to left

End	Middle	Beginning	Shape of Letter
ـض	ـضـ	ضـ	ض

ضي

ḍee

Long Vowel: Yaa

ضي	ضو	ضا	قَضِيب
ḍee	ḍoo	ḍaa	qaḍeeb - Rod
Long Vowel: Yaa	Long Vowel: Waw	Long Vowel: Alif	Ḍaad (ض) with long vowel Yaa sounds: 'Ḍee' — deep & long, with a wide smile

Read & write from right to left

End	Middle	Beginning	Shape of Letter
ـض	ـضـ	ضـ	ض

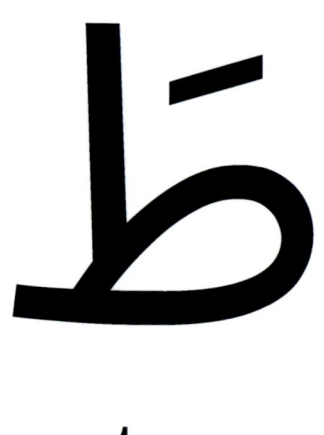

طَ

ṭa

Short Vowel: Fatḥa

طِ	طُ	طَ	طَيْر
ṭi	ṭo	ṭa	ṭayr - Bird
Short Vowel: Kasra	Short Vowel: Ḍammah	Short Vowel: Fatḥa	Ṭaa (ط) with Fatḥa sounds: 'Ṭa' — deep & short, with a slightly open mouth

Read & write from right to left

End	Middle	Beginning	Shape of Letter
ـط	ـطـ	طـ	ط

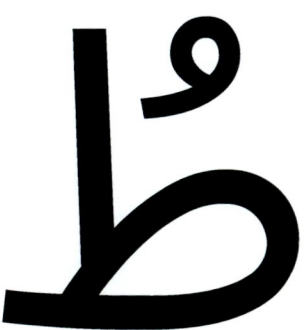

طُ

ṭo

Short Vowel: Ḍammah

طِ	طُ	طَ	طُلَّاب
ṭi	ṭo	ṭa	ṭollaab - Students
Short Vowel: Kasra	Short Vowel: Ḍammah	Short Vowel: Fatḥa	Ṭaa (ط) with Ḍammah sounds: 'Ṭo' — deep & short, with a rounded mouth

Read & write from right to left

End	Middle	Beginning	Shape of Letter
ـط	ـطـ	طـ	ط

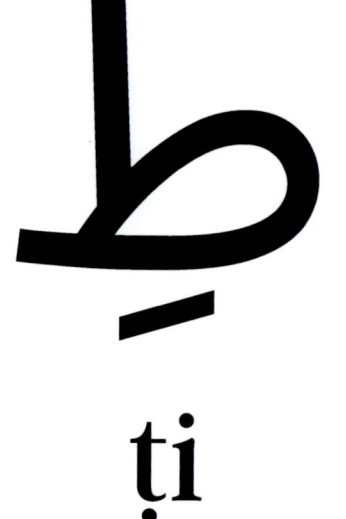

طِ

ṭi

Short Vowel: Kasra

طِ	طُ	طَ	طِفْل
ṭi	ṭo	ṭa	ṭifl - Child
Short Vowel: Kasra	Short Vowel: Ḍammah	Short Vowel: Fatḥa	Ṭaa (ط) with Kasra sounds: 'Ṭi' — deep & short, with a slight smile

Read & write from right to left

End	Middle	Beginning	Shape of Letter
ـط	ـطـ	طـ	ط

طا

ṭaa

Long Vowel: Alif

طي	طو	طا	طَائِرَة
ṭee	ṭoo	ṭaa	ṭaa-ira - Airplane
Long Vowel: Yaa	Long Vowel: Waw	Long Vowel: Alif	Ṭaa (ط) with long vowel Alif sounds: 'Ṭaa' — deep & long, with an open mouth

Read & write from right to left

End	Middle	Beginning	Shape of Letter
ـط	ـطـ	طـ	ط

طو

ṭoo

Long Vowel: Waw

طي	طو	طا	مَقْطُورَة
ṭee	ṭoo	ṭaa	maqṭoora - Trailer
Long Vowel: Yaa	Long Vowel: Waw	Long Vowel: Alif	Ṭaa (ط) with long vowel Waw sounds: 'Ṭoo' — deep & long, with a rounded mouth

Read & write from right to left

End	Middle	Beginning	Shape of Letter
ـط	ـطـ	طـ	ط

طي

ṭee

Long Vowel: Yaa

طي	طو	طا	طِين
ṭee	ṭoo	ṭaa	ṭeen - Mud
Long Vowel: Yaa	Long Vowel: Waw	Long Vowel: Alif	Ṭaa (ط) with long vowel Yaa sounds: 'Ṭee' — deep & long, with a wide smile

Read & write from right to left

End	Middle	Beginning	Shape of Letter
ـط	ـطـ	طـ	ط

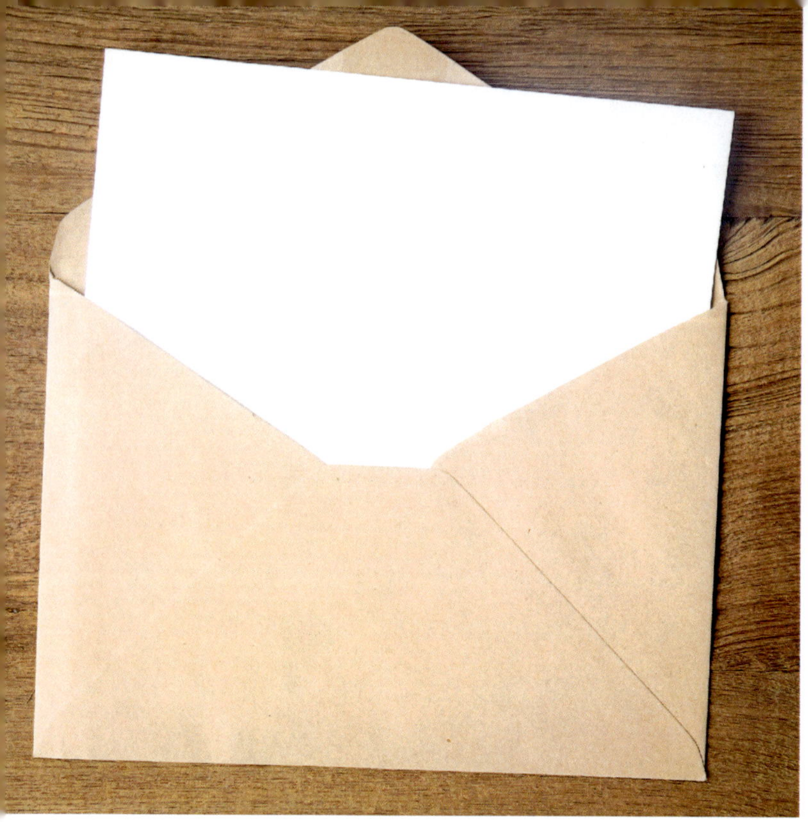

ظَ

ḍha

Short Vowel: Fatḥa

ظِ	ظُ	ظَ	ظَرْف
ḍhi	ḍho	ḍha	ḍharf - Envelope
Short Vowel: Kasra	Short Vowel: Ḍammah	Short Vowel: Fatḥa	Ḍhaa (ظ) with Fatḥa sounds: 'Ḍha' — deep & short, with a slightly open mouth

Read & write from right to left

End	Middle	Beginning	Shape of Letter
ـظ	ـظـ	ظـ	ظ

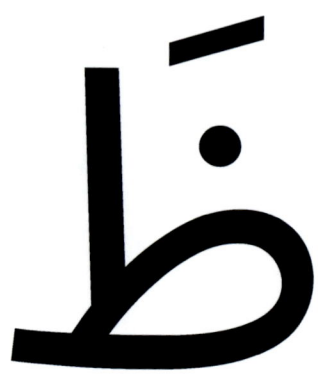

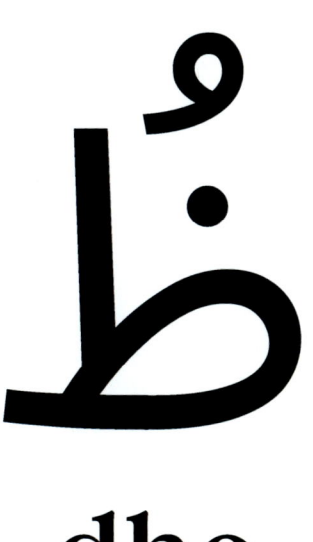

ظُ

ḍho

Short Vowel: Ḍammah

ظِ	ظُ	ظَ	ظُفْر
ḍhi	ḍho	ḍha	ḍhofr - Nail
Short Vowel: Kasra	Short Vowel: Ḍammah	Short Vowel: Fatḥa	Ḍhaa (ظ) with Ḍammah sounds: 'Ḍho' — deep & short, with a rounded mouth

Read & write from right to left

End	Middle	Beginning	Shape of Letter
ـظ	ـظـ	ظـ	ظ

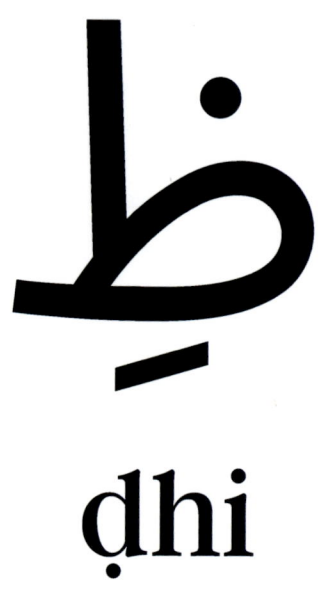

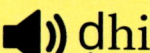

ظِ

ḍhi

Short Vowel: Kasra

ظِلّ

ḍhill - Shade or Shadow

Ḍhaa (ظ) with Kasra sounds: 'Ḍhi' — deep & short, with a slight smile

ظِ	ظُ	ظَ
ḍhi	ḍho	ḍha
Short Vowel: Kasra	Short Vowel: Ḍammah	Short Vowel: Fatḥa

Read & write from right to left

End	Middle	Beginning	Shape of Letter
ـظ	ـظـ	ظـ	ظ

ظا

ḍhaa

Long Vowel: Alif

ظي	ظو	ظا	مُظَاهَرَة
ḍhee	ḍhoo	ḍhaa	moḍhaahara - Protest
Long Vowel: Yaa	Long Vowel: Waw	Long Vowel: Alif	Ḍhaa (ظ) with long vowel Alif sounds: 'Ḍhaa' — deep & long, with an open mouth

Read & write from right to left

End	Middle	Beginning	Shape of Letter
ـظ	ـظـ	ظـ	ظ

ظو

ḍhoo

Long Vowel: Waw

ظي	ظو	ظا	مَحْظُور
ḍhee	ḍhoo	ḍhaa	maḥḍhoor - Restricted
Long Vowel: Yaa	Long Vowel: Waw	Long Vowel: Alif	Ḍhaa (ظ) with long vowel Waw sounds: 'Ḍhoo' — deep & long, with a rounded mouth

Read & write from right to left

End	Middle	Beginning	Shape of Letter
ـظ	ـظـ	ظـ	ظ

ظِي

ḍhee

Long Vowel: Yaa

وَظِيفَة

waḍheefa - Homework

Ḍhaa (ظ) with long vowel Yaa sounds: 'Ḍhee' — deep & long, with a wide smile

ظا	ظو	ظي
ḍhaa	ḍhoo	ḍhee
Long Vowel: Alif	Long Vowel: Waw	Long Vowel: Yaa

Read & write from right to left

Shape of Letter	Beginning	Middle	End
ظ	ظـ	ـظـ	ـظ

Beginning or when preceded by a one-way connecter letter

عَ

ʿa

Short Vowel: Fatḥa

عِ	عُ	عَ	عَسَل
ʿi	ʿo	ʿa	ʿasal - Honey
Short Vowel: Kasra	Short Vowel: Ḍammah	Short Vowel: Fatḥa	ʿAyn (ع) with Fatḥa sounds: “A’ — deep, throaty & short, like lifting something heavy, with a slightly open mouth (not in English)

Read & write from right to left

End	Middle	Beginning	Shape of Letter
ـع	ـعـ	عـ	ع

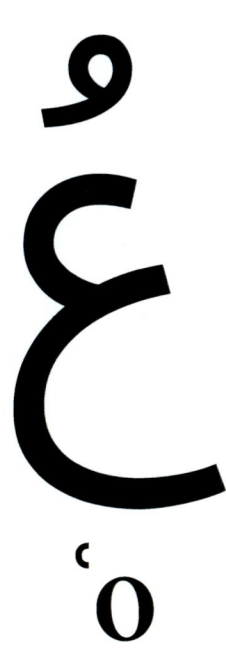

عُ

ʿo

Short Vowel: Ḍammah

عِ	عُ	عَ	عُشّ
ʿi	ʿo	ʿa	ʿosh - Nest
Short Vowel: Kasra	Short Vowel: Ḍammah	Short Vowel: Fatḥa	ʿAyn (ع) with Ḍammah sounds: "O' — deep, throaty & short, like lifting something heavy, with a rounded mouth (not in English)

Read & write from right to left

End	Middle	Beginning	Shape of Letter
ـع	ـعـ	عـ	ع

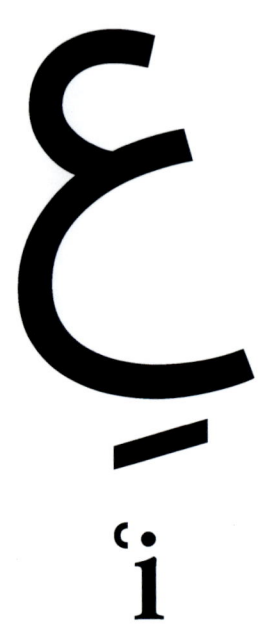

عِ

ʿi

Short Vowel: Kasra

عِنَب	عَ	عُ	عِ
ʿinab - Grape	ʿa	ʿo	ʿi
ʿAyn (ع) with Kasra sounds: "I' — deep, throaty & short, like lifting something heavy, with a slight smile (not in English)	Short Vowel: Fatḥa	Short Vowel: Ḍammah	Short Vowel: Kasra

Read & write from right to left

Shape of Letter	Beginning	Middle	End
ع	عـ	ـعـ	ـع

عا

ʿaa

Long Vowel: Alif

عي	عو	عا	عَائِلَة
ʿee	ʿoo	ʿaa	ʿaa-ila - Family
Long Vowel: Yaa	Long Vowel: Waw	Long Vowel: Alif	ʿAyn (ع) with long vowel Alif sounds: "Aa' — deep, throaty & long, like lifting something heavy, with an open mouth (not in English)

Read & write from right to left

End	Middle	Beginning	Shape of Letter
ـع	ـعـ	عـ	ع

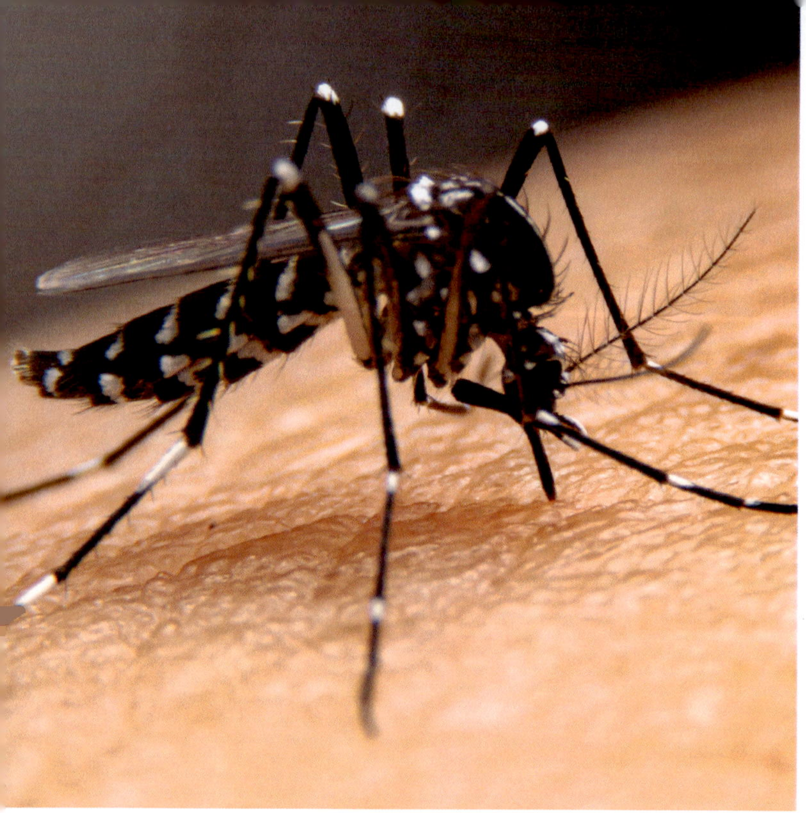

عو

ʿoo

Long Vowel: Waw

عي	عو	عا	بَعُوض
ʿee	ʿoo	ʿaa	baʿooḍ - Mosquito
Long Vowel: Yaa	Long Vowel: Waw	Long Vowel: Alif	ʿAyn (ع) with long vowel Waw sounds: "Oo' — deep, throaty & long, like lifting something heavy, with a rounded mouth (not in English)

Read & write from right to left

End	Middle	Beginning	Shape of Letter
ـع	ـعـ	عـ	ع

عي

ʿee

Long Vowel: Yaa

عي	عو	عا	سَعِيد
ʿee	ʿoo	ʿaa	sa-ʿeed - Happy
Long Vowel: Yaa	Long Vowel: Waw	Long Vowel: Alif	ʿAyn (ع) with long vowel Yaa sounds: "Ee' — deep, throaty & long, like lifting something heavy, with a wide smile (not in English)

Read & write from right to left

End	Middle	Beginning	Shape of Letter
ـع	ـعـ	عـ	ع

غَ

gha

Short Vowel: Fatḥa

غِ	غُ	غَ	غَزَال
ghi	gho	gha	ghazal - Deer
Short Vowel: Kasra	Short Vowel: Ḍammah	Short Vowel: Fatḥa	Ghayn (غ) with Fatḥa sounds: 'Gha' — deep, throaty & short, with vibration, like gargling, with a slightly open mouth (not in English)

Read & write from right to left

End	Middle	Beginning	Shape of Letter
ـغ	ـغـ	غـ	غ

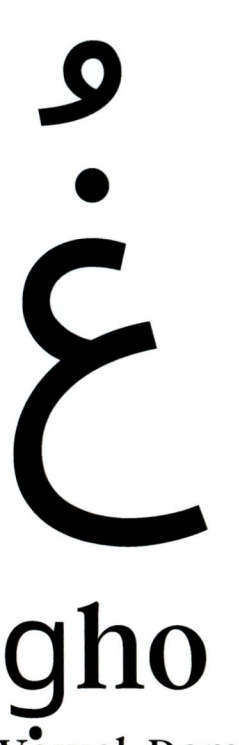

غُ

gho

Short Vowel: Ḍammah

غِ	غُ	غَ	غُرَاب
ghi	gho	gha	ghoraab - Crow
Short Vowel: Kasra	Short Vowel: Ḍammah	Short Vowel: Fatḥa	Ghayn (غ) with Ḍammah sounds: 'Gho' — deep, throaty & short, with vibration, like gargling, with a rounded mouth (not in English)

Read & write from right to left

End	Middle	Beginning	Shape of Letter
ـغ	ـغـ	غـ	غ

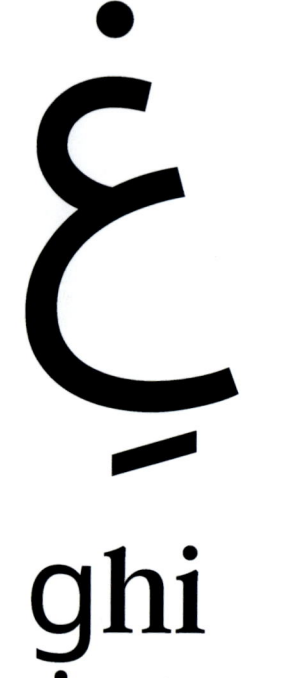

غِ

ghi

Short Vowel: Kasra

غِ	غُ	غَ	غِنَاء
ghi	gho	gha	ghinaa - Singing
Short Vowel: Kasra	Short Vowel: Ḍammah	Short Vowel: Fatḥa	Ghayn (غ) with Kasra sounds: 'Ghi' — deep, throaty & short, with vibration, like gargling, with a slight smile (not in English)

Read & write from right to left

End	Middle	Beginning	Shape of Letter
ـغ	ـغـ	غـ	غ

غا

ghaa

Long Vowel: Alif

غي	غو	غا	غَابَة
ghee	ghoo	ghaa	ghaaba - Forest
Long Vowel: Yaa	Long Vowel: Waw	Long Vowel: Alif	Ghayn (غ) with long vowel Alif sounds: 'Ghaa' — deep, throaty & long, with vibration, like gargling, with an open mouth (not in English)

Read & write from right to left

End	Middle	Beginning	Shape of Letter
ـغ	ـغـ	غـ	غ

غو

ghoo

Long Vowel: Waw

غي	غو	غا	يَغُوص
ghee	ghoo	ghaa	yaghooṣ - To Dive
Long Vowel: Yaa	Long Vowel: Waw	Long Vowel: Alif	Ghayn (غ) with long vowel Waw sounds: 'Ghoo' — deep, throaty & long, with vibration, like gargling, with a rounded mouth (not in English)

Read & write from right to left

End	Middle	Beginning	Shape of Letter
ـغ	ـغـ	غـ	غ

غي

ghee

Long Vowel: Yaa

غي	غو	غا	صَغِير
ghee	ghoo	ghaa	ṣagheer - Small
Long Vowel: Yaa	Long Vowel: Waw	Long Vowel: Alif	Ghayn (غ) with long vowel Yaa sounds: 'Ghee' — deep, throaty & long, with vibration, like gargling, with a wide smile (not in English)

Read & write from right to left

End	Middle	Beginning	Shape of Letter
ـغ	ـغـ	غـ	غ

فَ

fa

Short Vowel: Fatḥa

فِ	فُ	فَ	فَرَاشَة
fi	fo	fa	faraasha - Butterfly
Short Vowel: Kasra	Short Vowel: Ḍammah	Short Vowel: Fatḥa	Faa (ف) with Fatḥa sounds: 'Fa' — light & short, with a slightly open mouth

Read & write from right to left

End	Middle	Beginning	Shape of Letter
ـف	ـفـ	فـ	ف

فُ

fo

Short Vowel: Ḍammah

فِ	فُ	فَ	فُندُق
fi	fo	fa	fondoq - Hotel
Short Vowel: Kasra	Short Vowel: Ḍammah	Short Vowel: Fatḥa	Faa (ف) with Ḍammah sounds: 'Fo' — light & short, with a rounded mouth

Read & write from right to left

End	Middle	Beginning	Shape of Letter
ـف	ـفـ	فـ	ف

فِ

fi

Short Vowel: Kasra

فِ	فُ	فَ	فِكْرَة
fi	fo	fa	fikrah - Idea
Short Vowel: Kasra	Short Vowel: Ḍammah	Short Vowel: Fatḥa	Faa (ف) with Kasra sounds: 'Fi' — light & short, with a slight smile

Read & write from right to left

End	Middle	Beginning	Shape of Letter
ـف	ـفـ	فـ	ف

فا

faa

Long Vowel: Alif

في	فو	فا	فَارِس
fee	foo	faa	faris - Horseman
Long Vowel: Yaa	Long Vowel: Waw	Long Vowel: Alif	Faa (ف) with long vowel Alif sounds: 'Faa' — light & long, with an open mouth

← - - - - - - - - - - - - - - Read & write from right to left ← - - - - - - - - - - - - - -

End	Middle	Beginning	Shape of Letter
ـف	ـفـ	فـ	ف

فو

foo

Long Vowel: Waw

في	فو	فا	فُول
fee	foo	faa	fool - Fava Beans
Long Vowel: Yaa	Long Vowel: Waw	Long Vowel: Alif	Faa (ف) with long vowel Waw sounds: 'Foo' — light & long, with a rounded mouth

Read & write from right to left

End	Middle	Beginning	Shape of Letter
ـف	ـفـ	فـ	ف

في

fee

Long Vowel: Yaa

في	فو	فا	فِيل
fee	foo	faa	feel - Elephant
Long Vowel: Yaa	Long Vowel: Waw	Long Vowel: Alif	Faa (ف) with long vowel Yaa sounds: 'Fee' — light & long, with a wide smile

Read & write from right to left

End	Middle	Beginning	Shape of Letter
ـف	ـفـ	فـ	ف

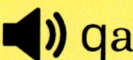

قَ

qa

Short Vowel: Fatḥa

قِ	قُ	قَ	قَمَر
qi	qo	qa	qamar - Moon
Short Vowel: Kasra	Short Vowel: Ḍammah	Short Vowel: Fatḥa	Qaaf (ق) with Fatḥa sounds: 'Qa' — deep, throaty & short, with a slightly open mouth

Read & write from right to left

End	Middle	Beginning	Shape of Letter
ـق	ـقـ	قـ	ق

قُ

qo

Short Vowel: Ḍammah

قِ	قُ	قَ	قُبْطَان
qi	qo	qa	qobṭaan - Captain
Short Vowel: Kasra	Short Vowel: Ḍammah	Short Vowel: Fatḥa	Qaaf (ق) with Ḍammah sounds: 'Qo' — deep, throaty & short, with a rounded mouth

Read & write from right to left

End	Middle	Beginning	Shape of Letter
ـق	ـقـ	قـ	ق

قِ

qi

Short Vowel: Kasra

قِطَّة	قَ	قُ	قِ
qiṭṭa - Cat	qa	qo	qi
Qaaf (ق) with Kasra sounds: 'Qi' — deep, throaty & short, with a slight smile	Short Vowel: Fatḥa	Short Vowel: Ḍammah	Short Vowel: Kasra

Read & write from right to left

Shape of Letter	Beginning	Middle	End
ق	قـ	ـقـ	ـق

قا

qaa

Long Vowel: Alif

قي	قو	قا	فُقَّاعَة
qee	qoo	qaa	foqqaʿa - Bubble
Long Vowel: Yaa	Long Vowel: Waw	Long Vowel: Alif	Qaaf (ق) with long vowel Alif sounds: 'Qaa' — deep, throaty & long, with an open mouth

Read & write from right to left

End	Middle	Beginning	Shape of Letter
ـق	ـقـ	قـ	ق

قو

qoo

Long Vowel: Waw

قي	قو	قا	سُقُوط
qee	🔊 qoo	qaa	soqooṭ - Falling
Long Vowel: Yaa	Long Vowel: Waw	Long Vowel: Alif	Qaaf (ق) with long vowel Waw sounds: 'Qoo' — deep, throaty & long, with a rounded mouth

← - - - - - - - - - - - - - - Read & write from right to left ← - - - - - - - - - - - - - -

End	Middle	Beginning	Shape of Letter
ـق	ـقـ	قـ	ق

قِي

qee

Long Vowel: Yaa

قِي	قُو	قَا	دَقِيق
qee	qoo	qaa	daqeeq- Flour
Long Vowel: Yaa	Long Vowel: Waw	Long Vowel: Alif	Qaaf (ق) with long vowel Yaa sounds: 'Qee' — deep, throaty & long, with a wide smile

Read & write from right to left

End	Middle	Beginning	Shape of Letter
ـق	ـقـ	قـ	ق

Beginning or when preceded by a one-way connecter letter

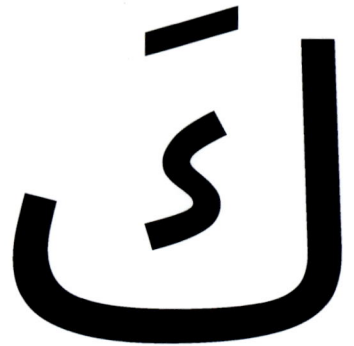

كَ

ka

Short Vowel: Fatḥa

كِ	كُ	كَ	كَلْب
ki	ko	ka	kalb - Dog
Short Vowel: Kasra	Short Vowel: Ḍammah	Short Vowel: Fatḥa	Kaaf (ك) with Fatḥa sounds: 'Ka' — light & short, with a slightly open mouth

Read & write from right to left

End	Middle	Beginning	Shape of Letter
ـك	ـكـ	كـ	ك

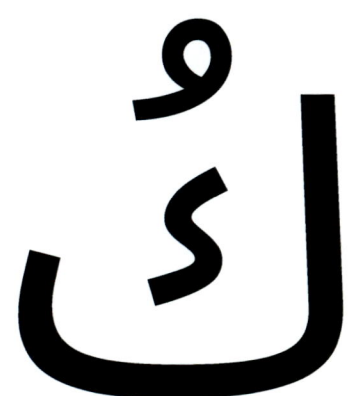

كُ

ko

Short Vowel: Ḍammah

كِ	كُ	كَ	كُرَة
ki	ko	ka	Kora - Ball
Short Vowel: Kasra	Short Vowel: Ḍammah	Short Vowel: Fatḥa	Kaaf (ك) with Ḍammah sounds: 'Ko' — light & short, with a rounded mouth

Read & write from right to left

End	Middle	Beginning	Shape of Letter
ـك	ـكـ	كـ	ك

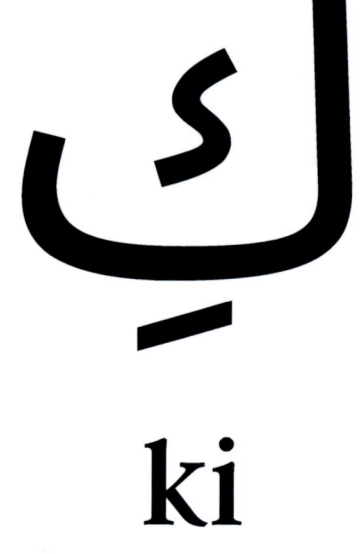

كِ

ki

Short Vowel: Kasra

كِ	كُ	كَ	كِتَاب
ki	ko	ka	kitaab - Book
Short Vowel: Kasra	Short Vowel: Ḍammah	Short Vowel: Fatḥa	Kaaf (ك) with Kasra sounds: 'Ki' — light & short, with a slight smile

Read & write from right to left

End	Middle	Beginning	Shape of Letter
ـك	ـكـ	كـ	ك

كا

kaa

Long Vowel: Alif

كي	كو	كا	كَاتِب
kee	koo	kaa	kaatib - Writer
Long Vowel: Yaa	Long Vowel: Waw	Long Vowel: Alif	Kaaf (ك) with long vowel Alif sounds: 'Kaa' — light & long, with an open mouth

Read & write from right to left

End	Middle	Beginning	Shape of Letter
ـك	ـكـ	كـ	ك

كو

koo

Long Vowel: Waw

كي	كو	كا	كُوخ
kee	koo	kaa	kooḳh - Hut
Long Vowel: Yaa	Long Vowel: Waw	Long Vowel: Alif	Kaaf (ك) with long vowel Waw sounds: 'Koo' — light & long, with a rounded mouth

← - - - - - - - - - - - - - - Read & write from right to left ← - - - - - - - - - - - - - -

End	Middle	Beginning	Shape of Letter
ـك	ـكـ	كـ	ك

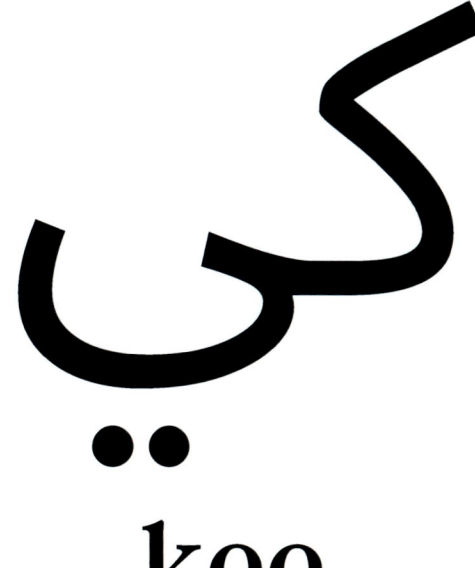

كِي

kee

Long Vowel: Yaa

كِي	كُو	كَا	حَكِيم
kee	koo	kaa	ḥakeem - Doctor
Long Vowel: Yaa	Long Vowel: Waw	Long Vowel: Alif	Kaaf (ك) with long vowel Yaa sounds: 'Kee' — light & long, with a wide smile

Read & write from right to left

End	Middle	Beginning	Shape of Letter
ـك	ـكـ	كـ	ك

لَ

la

Short Vowel: Fatḥa

لِ	لُ	لَ	لَبَن
li	lo	la	laban - Yogurt
Short Vowel: Kasra	Short Vowel: Ḍammah	Short Vowel: Fatḥa	Laam (ل) with Fatḥa sounds: 'La' — light & short, with a slightly open mouth

Read & write from right to left

End	Middle	Beginning	Shape of Letter
ـل	ـلـ	لـ	ل

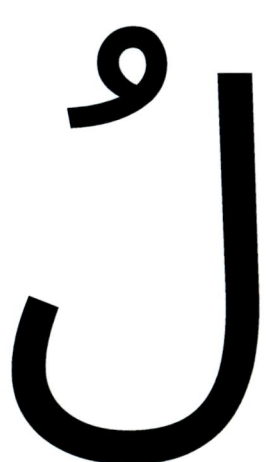

لُ

lo

Short Vowel: Ḍammah

لِ	لُ	لَ	لُؤْلُؤ
li	lo	la	lo-lo - Pearl
Short Vowel: Kasra	Short Vowel: Ḍammah	Short Vowel: Fatḥa	Laam (ل) with Ḍammah sounds: 'Lo' — light & short, with a rounded mouth

Read & write from right to left

End	Middle	Beginning	Shape of Letter
ـل	ـلـ	لـ	ل

Beginning or when preceded by a one-way connecter letter

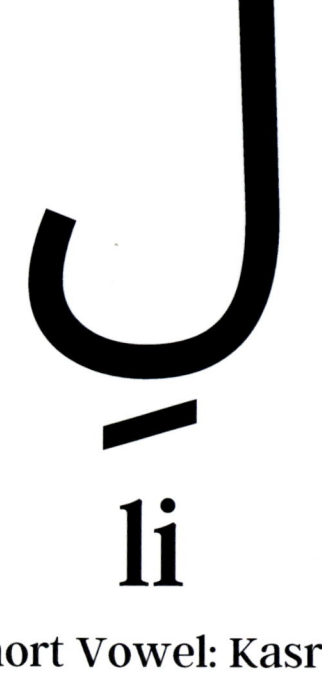

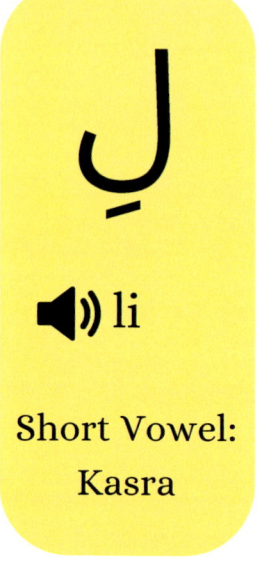

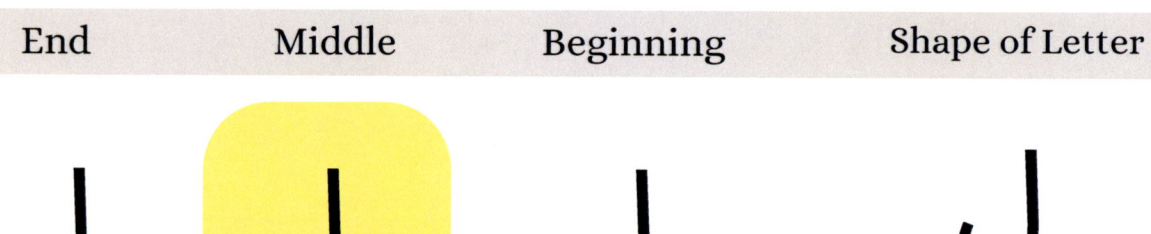

لِ

li

Short Vowel: Kasra

لِ	لُ	لَ	مَلِك
li	lo	la	malik - King
Short Vowel: Kasra	Short Vowel: Ḍammah	Short Vowel: Fatḥa	Laam (ل) with Kasra sounds: 'Li' — light & short, with a slight smile

Read & write from right to left

End	Middle	Beginning	Shape of Letter
ـل	ـلـ	لـ	ل

لا

laa

Long Vowel: Alif

لي	لو	لا	لَا
lee	loo	laa	laa - No
Long Vowel: Yaa	Long Vowel: Waw	Long Vowel: Alif	Laam (ل) with long vowel Alif sounds: 'Laa' — light & long, with an open mouth

←-------------- Read & write from right to left ←--------------

End	Middle	Beginning	Shape of Letter
ـل	ـلـ	لـ	ل

لو

loo

Long Vowel: Waw

لي	لو	لا	دَلُو
lee	loo	laa	daloo - Bucket
Long Vowel: Yaa	Long Vowel: Waw	Long Vowel: Alif	Laam (ل) with long vowel Waw sounds: 'Loo' — light & long, with a rounded mouth

Read & write from right to left

End	Middle	Beginning	Shape of Letter
ـل	ـلـ	لـ	ل

Beginning or when preceded by a one-way connecter letter

لي

lee

Long Vowel: Yaa

لي	لو	لا	جَلِيد
lee	loo	laa	jaleed - Ice
Long Vowel: Yaa	Long Vowel: Waw	Long Vowel: Alif	Laam (ل) with long vowel Yaa sounds: 'Lee' – light & long, with a wide smile

Read & write from right to left

End	Middle	Beginning	Shape of Letter
ـل	ـلـ	لـ	ل

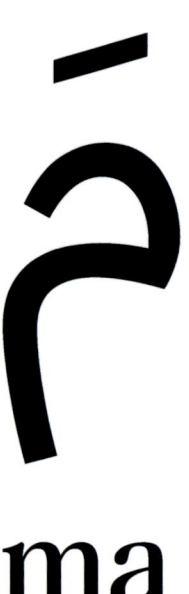

مَ

ma

Short Vowel: Fatḥa

مِ	مُ	مَ	مَوْز
mi	mo	ma	maws - Banana
Short Vowel: Kasra	Short Vowel: Ḍammah	Short Vowel: Fatḥa	Meem (م) with Fatḥa sounds: ‘Ma’ — light & short, with a slightly open mouth

Read & write from right to left

End	Middle	Beginning	Shape of Letter
ـم	ـمـ	مـ	م

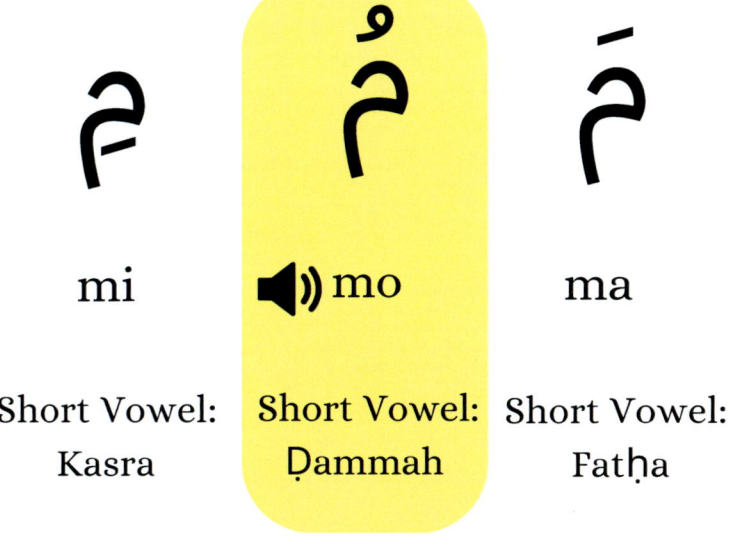

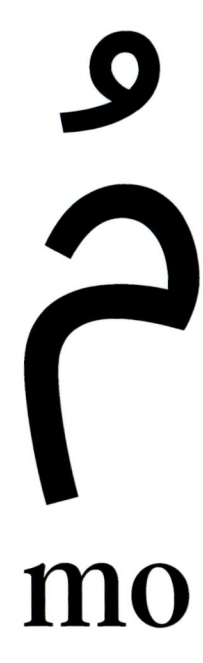

مُ

mo

Short Vowel: Ḍammah

مِ	مُ	مَ	مُرْجَان
mi	mo	ma	morjaan - Coral
Short Vowel: Kasra	Short Vowel: Ḍammah	Short Vowel: Fatḥa	Meem (م) with Ḍammah sounds: 'Mo' — light & short, with a rounded mouth

Read & write from right to left

End	Middle	Beginning	Shape of Letter
ـم	ـمـ	مـ	م

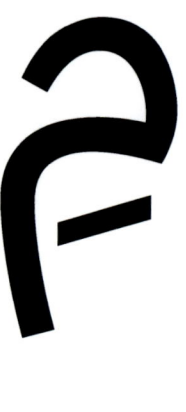

مِ

mi

Short Vowel: Kasra

مِ	مُ	مَ	مِرْآة
mi	mo	ma	mir-aa - Mirror
Short Vowel: Kasra	Short Vowel: Ḍammah	Short Vowel: Fatḥa	Meem (م) with Kasra sounds: 'Mi' — light & short, with a slight smile

Read & write from right to left

End	Middle	Beginning	Shape of Letter
ـم	ـمـ	مـ	م

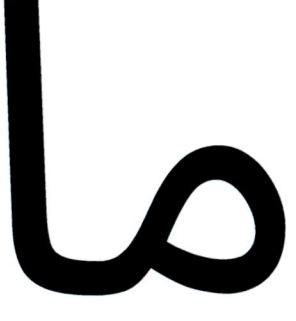

ما

maa

Long Vowel: Alif

مي	مو	ما	مَاعِز
mee	moo	maa	maaʿis - Goat
Long Vowel: Yaa	Long Vowel: Waw	Long Vowel: Alif	Meem (م) with long vowel Alif sounds: 'Maa' — light & long, with an open mouth

Read & write from right to left

End	Middle	Beginning	Shape of Letter
ـم	ـمـ	مـ	م

مو

moo

Long Vowel: Waw

مُوسِيقَى

mooseeqa - Music

Meem (م) with long vowel Waw sounds: 'Moo' – light & long, with a rounded mouth

ما

maa

Long Vowel: Alif

مو

moo

Long Vowel: Waw

مي

mee

Long Vowel: Yaa

Read & write from right to left

End	Middle	Beginning	Shape of Letter
ـم	ـمـ	مـ	م

مي

mee

Long Vowel: Yaa

مي	مو	ما	مِينَاء
mee	moo	maa	meenaa - Port
Long Vowel: Yaa	Long Vowel: Waw	Long Vowel: Alif	Meem (م) with long vowel Yaa sounds: 'Mee' — light & long, with a wide smile

Read & write from right to left

End	Middle	Beginning	Shape of Letter
ـم	ـمـ	مـ	م

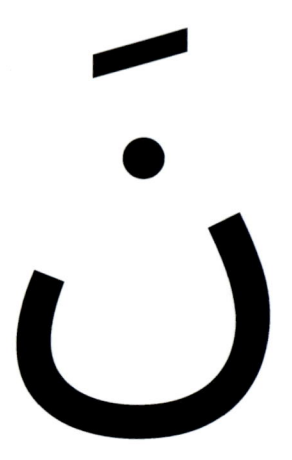

نَ

na

Short Vowel: Fatḥa

نِ	نُ	نَ	نَحْلَة
ni	no	na	naḥla - Bee
Short Vowel: Kasra	Short Vowel: Ḍammah	Short Vowel: Fatḥa	Noon (ن) with Fatḥa sounds: 'Na' — light & short, with a slightly open mouth

Read & write from right to left

End	Middle	Beginning	Shape of Letter
ـن	ـنـ	نـ	ن

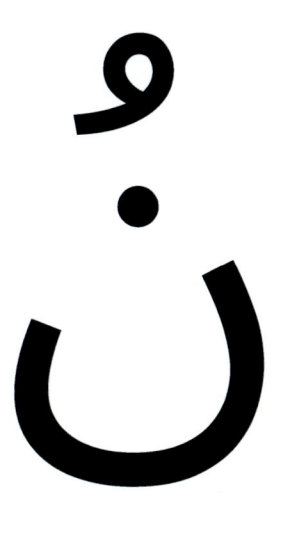

نُ

no

Short Vowel: Ḍammah

نِ	نُ	نَ	نُزْهَة
ni	no	na	nozha - Picnic
Short Vowel: Kasra	Short Vowel: Ḍammah	Short Vowel: Fatḥa	Noon (ن) with Ḍammah sounds: 'No' — light & short, with a rounded mouth

Read & write from right to left

End	Middle	Beginning	Shape of Letter
ـن	ـنـ	نـ	ن

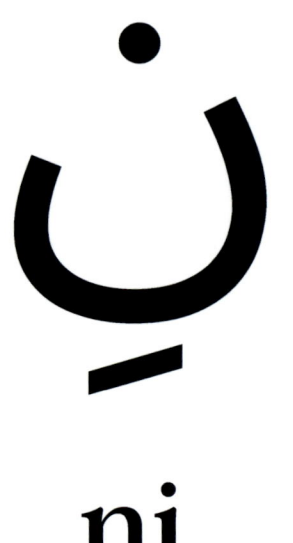

نِ

ni

Short Vowel: Kasra

نِ	نُ	نَ	نِسْر
ni	no	na	nisr - Eagle
Short Vowel: Kasra	Short Vowel: Ḍammah	Short Vowel: Fatḥa	Noon (ن) with Kasra sounds: 'Ni' — light & short, with a slight smile

Read & write from right to left

End	Middle	Beginning	Shape of Letter
ـن	ـنـ	نـ	ن

نا

naa

Long Vowel: Alif

نِي	نُو	نا	نَار
nee	noo	naa	naar - Fire
Long Vowel: Yaa	Long Vowel: Waw	Long Vowel: Alif	Noon (ن) with long vowel Alif sounds: 'Naa' — light & long, with an open mouth

Read & write from right to left

End	Middle	Beginning	Shape of Letter
ـن	ـنـ	نـ	ن

نو

noo

Long Vowel: Waw

ني	نو	نا	نُور
nee	noo	naa	noor - Light
Long Vowel: Yaa	Long Vowel: Waw	Long Vowel: Alif	Noon (ن) with long vowel Waw sounds: 'Noo' — light & long, with a rounded mouth

Read & write from right to left

End	Middle	Beginning	Shape of Letter
ـن	ـنـ	نـ	ن

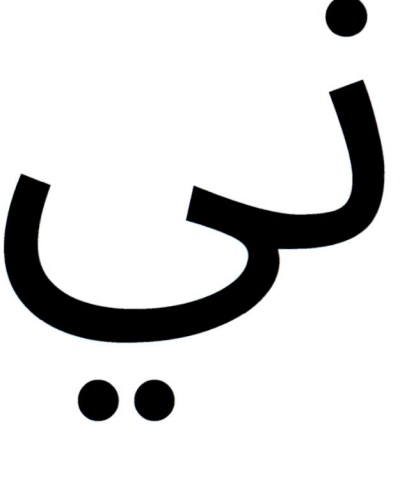

ني

nee

Long Vowel: Yaa

ني	نو	نا	رَنِين
nee	noo	naa	raneen - Ringing
Long Vowel: Yaa	Long Vowel: Waw	Long Vowel: Alif	Noon (ن) with long vowel Yaa sounds: 'Nee' — light & long, with a wide smile

Read & write from right to left

End	Middle	Beginning	Shape of Letter
ـن	ـنـ	نـ	ن

Beginning or when preceded by a one-way connecter letter

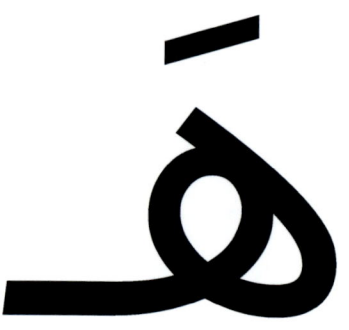

هَـ

ha

Short Vowel: Fatḥa

هِـ	هُـ	هَـ	هَدِيَّة
hi	ho	ha	hadiyya - Gift
Short Vowel: Kasra	Short Vowel: Ḍammah	Short Vowel: Fatḥa	Haa (هـ) with Fatḥa sounds: 'Ha' – light & short, with a slightly open mouth

Read & write from right to left

End	Middle	Beginning	Shape of Letter
ـه	ـهـ	هـ	هـ

! Or, as an isolated loop (ه) when preceded by a one-way connector at the end

هُـ

ho

Short Vowel: Ḍammah

هِـ	هُـ	هَـ	هُدُوء
hi	ho	ha	hodoo - Silence
Short Vowel: Kasra	Short Vowel: Ḍammah	Short Vowel: Fatḥa	Haa (هـ) with Ḍammah sounds: 'Ho' — light & short, with a rounded mouth

Read & write from right to left

End	Middle	Beginning	Shape of Letter
ـه	ـهـ	هـ	هـ

! Or, as an isolated loop (ه) when preceded by a one-way connector at the end

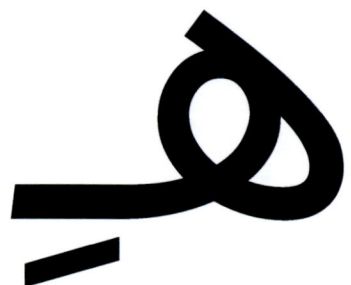

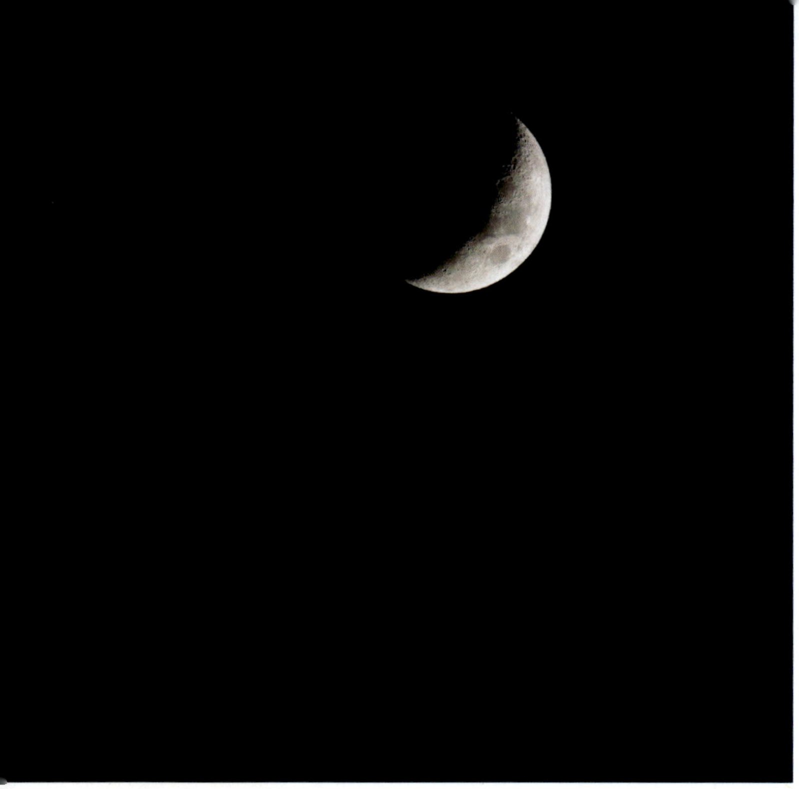

هِـ

hi

Short Vowel: Kasra

هِـ	هُـ	هَـ	هِلَال
hi	ho	ha	hilaal - Crescent
Short Vowel: Kasra	Short Vowel: Ḍammah	Short Vowel: Fatḥa	Haa (هـ) with Kasra sounds: 'Hi' — light & short, with a slight smile

Read & write from right to left

End	Middle	Beginning	Shape of Letter
ـه	ـهـ	هـ	هـ

Or, as an isolated loop (ه) when preceded by a one-way connector at the end

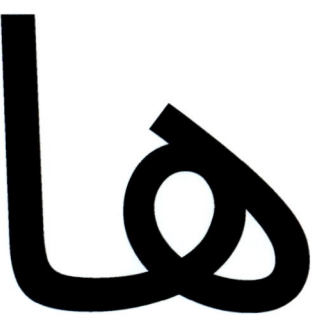

ها

haa

Long Vowel: Alif

هي	هو	ها	شِهَاب
hee	hoo	haa	shihaab - Shooting Star
Long Vowel: Yaa	Long Vowel: Waw	Long Vowel: Alif	Haa (هـ) with long vowel Alif sounds: 'Haa' — light & long, with an open mouth

Read & write from right to left

End	Middle	Beginning	Shape of Letter
ـه	ـهـ	هـ	هـ

Or, as an isolated loop (ه) when preceded by a one-way connector at the end

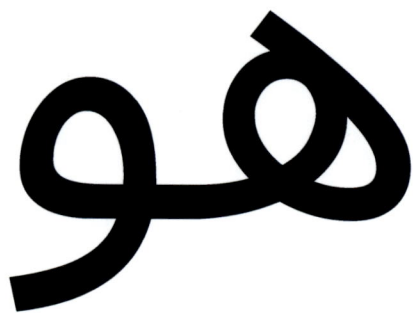

هو

hoo

Long Vowel: Waw

هـي	هو	ها	سُهُول
hee	hoo	haa	sohool - Plains
Long Vowel: Yaa	Long Vowel: Waw	Long Vowel: Alif	Haa (هـ) with long vowel Waw sounds: 'Hoo' — light & long, with a rounded mouth

Read & write from right to left

End	Middle	Beginning	Shape of Letter
ـه	ـهـ	هـ	هـ

Or, as an isolated loop (ه) when preceded by a one-way connector at the end

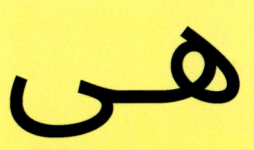

هــي

hee

Long Vowel: Yaa

هــي	هو	ها	بَهِيج
hee	hoo	haa	baheej - Festive
Long Vowel: Yaa	Long Vowel: Waw	Long Vowel: Alif	Haa (هـ) with long vowel Yaa sounds: 'Hee' — light & long, with a wide smile

Read & write from right to left

End	Middle	Beginning	Shape of Letter
ـه	ـهـ	هـ	هـ

Or, as an isolated loop (ه) when preceded by a one-way connector at the end

وَ

wa

Short Vowel: Fatḥa

وِ	وُ	وَ	وَلَد
wi	wo	wa	walad - Boy
Short Vowel: Kasra	Short Vowel: Ḍammah	Short Vowel: Fatḥa	Waw (و) with Fatḥa sounds: 'Wa' — light & short, with a slightly open mouth

Read & write from right to left

End	Middle	Beginning	Shape of Letter
ـو	ـو	و	و

وُ

WO

Short Vowel: Ḍammah

وِ	وُ	وَ	تَسَوُّق
wi	wo	wa	tasawwoq - Shopping
Short Vowel: Kasra	Short Vowel: Ḍammah	Short Vowel: Fatḥa	Waw (و) with Ḍammah sounds: 'Wo' — light & short, with a rounded mouth

Read & write from right to left

End	Middle	Beginning	Shape of Letter
ـو	ـو	و	و

وِ

wi

Short Vowel: Kasra

وِ	وُ	وَ	وِعَاء
wi	wo	wa	wiʿaa - Bowl
Short Vowel: Kasra	Short Vowel: Ḍammah	Short Vowel: Fatḥa	Waw (و) with Kasra sounds: 'Wi' — light & short, with a slight smile

Read & write from right to left

End	Middle	Beginning	Shape of Letter
ـو	ـو	و	و

وا

waa

Long Vowel: Alif

وي	وو	وا	وَادِي
wee	woo	waa	waadee - Valley
Long Vowel: Yaa	Long Vowel: Waw	Long Vowel: Alif	Waw (و) with long vowel Alif sounds: 'Waa' — light & long, with an open mouth

←-------------- Read & write from right to left ←--------------

End	Middle	Beginning	Shape of Letter
ـو	ـو	و	و

وو

woo

Long Vowel: Waw

وي	وو	وا	طَاوُوس
wee	woo	waa	ṭaawoos - Peacock
Long Vowel: Yaa	Long Vowel: Waw	Long Vowel: Alif	Waw (و) with long vowel Waw sounds: 'Woo' — light & long, with a rounded mouth

Read & write from right to left

End	Middle	Beginning	Shape of Letter
ـو	ـو	و	و

Beginning or when preceded by a one-way connecter letter

وي

wee

Long Vowel: Yaa

وي	وو	وا	تَلْوِين
wee	woo	waa	talween - Coloring
Long Vowel: Yaa	Long Vowel: Waw	Long Vowel: Alif	Waw (و) with long vowel Yaa sounds: 'Wee' — light & long, with a wide smile

← - - - - - - - - - - - - - - Read & write from right to left ← - - - - - - - - - - - - - -

End	Middle	Beginning	Shape of Letter
ـو	ـو	و	و

يَ

ya

Short Vowel: Fatḥa

يِ	يُ	يَ	يَقْطِين
yi	yo	ya	yaqṭeen - Pumpkin
Short Vowel: Kasra	Short Vowel: Ḍammah	Short Vowel: Fatḥa	Yaa (ي) with Fatḥa sounds: 'Ya' — light & short, with a slightly open mouth

Read & write from right to left

End	Middle	Beginning	Shape of Letter
ـي	ـيـ	يـ	ي

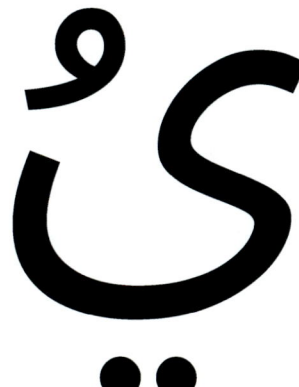

يُ

yo

Short Vowel: Ḍammah

يِ	يُ	يَ	يُسَاعِد
yi	yo	ya	yosaa-ʿid - To Assist
Short Vowel: Kasra	Short Vowel: Ḍammah	Short Vowel: Fatḥa	Yaa (ي) with Ḍammah sounds: 'Yo' — light & short, with a rounded mouth

Read & write from right to left

End	Middle	Beginning	Shape of Letter
ـي	ـيـ	يـ	ي

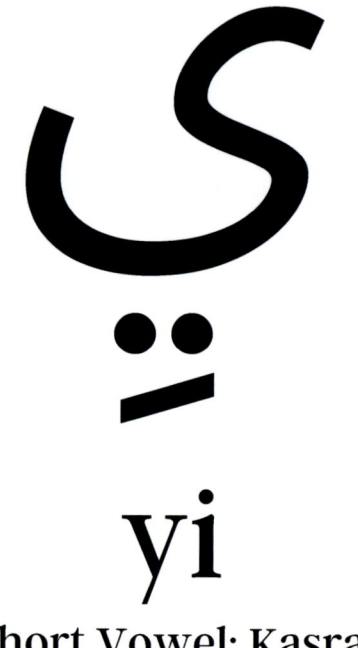

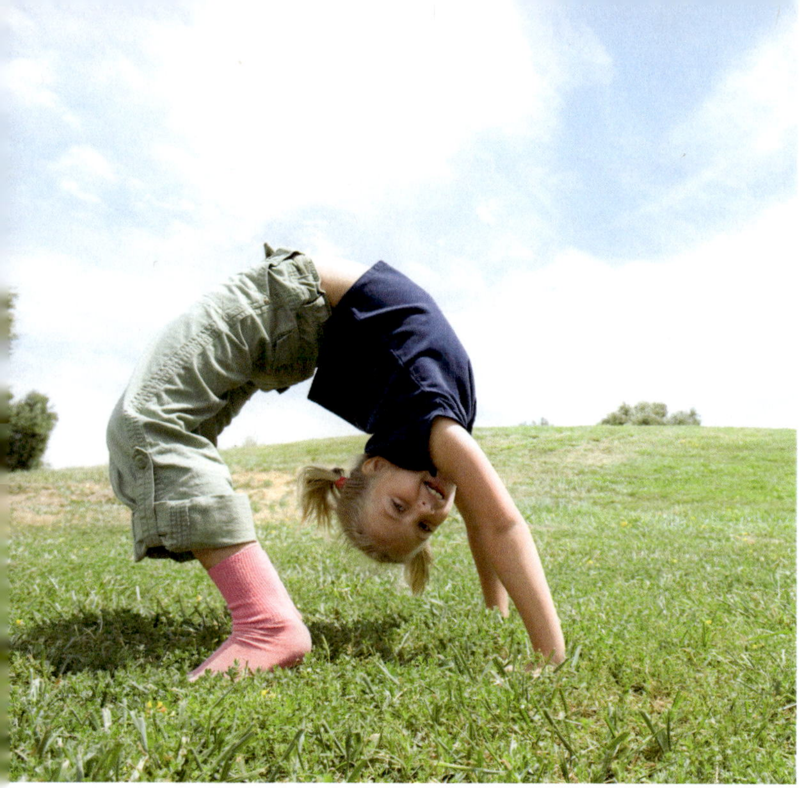

يِ

yi

Short Vowel: Kasra

يِ	يُ	يَ	لَيِّن
yi	yo	ya	layyin - Flexible
Short Vowel: Kasra	Short Vowel: Ḍammah	Short Vowel: Fatḥa	Yaa (ي) with Kasra sounds: 'Yi' — light & short, with a slight smile

Read & write from right to left

End	Middle	Beginning	Shape of Letter
ـي	ـيـ	يـ	ي

يا

yaa

Long Vowel: Alif

سَيَّارَة	يا	يو	يي
sayyara - Car	yaa	yoo	yee
Yaa (ي) with long vowel Alif sounds: 'Yaa' — light & long, with an open mouth	Long Vowel: Alif	Long Vowel: Waw	Long Vowel: Yaa

Read & write from right to left

Shape of Letter	Beginning	Middle	End
ي	يـ	ـيـ	ـي

يو

yoo

Long Vowel: Waw

يي	يو	يا	بُيُوت
yee	yoo	yaa	boyoot - Homes
Long Vowel: Yaa	Long Vowel: Waw	Long Vowel: Alif	Yaa (ي) with long vowel Waw sounds: 'Yoo' — light & long, with a rounded mouth

Read & write from right to left

End	Middle	Beginning	Shape of Letter
ـي	ـيـ	يـ	ي

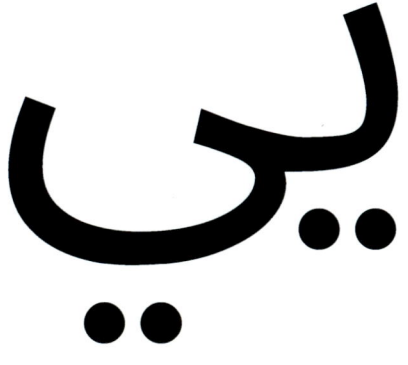

يي

yee

Long Vowel:Yaa

يي	يو	يا	تَخِيم
yee	yoo	yaa	taḳhyeem - Camping
Long Vowel: Yaa	Long Vowel: Waw	Long Vowel: Alif	Yaa (ي) with long vowel Yaa sounds: 'Yee' — light & long, with a wide smile

Read & write from right to left

End	Middle	Beginning	Shape of Letter
ـي	ـيـ	يـ	ي

Additional Practice:

طالِبَة ṭaaliba Student (female)	طالِب ṭaalib Student (male)	بَيْت bayt House	مَدْرَسَة madrasa School
أُسْتاذَة ostaadha Teacher (female)	أُسْتاذ ostaadh Teacher (male)	قَلَم qalam Pen	مَركَبَة markaba Vehicle
نافِذَة naafidha Window	قِطّة qiṭṭa Cat	طاوِلَة ṭaawila Table	كُرْسيّ korsiy Chair
شَراب sharaab Drink/Beverage	ماء maa' Water	طَعام ṭaʿaam Food	حافِلَة ḥaafila Bus
حَشَرات ḥasharaat Bugs	قَهْوَة qahwa Coffee	شاي shaai Tea	شَمْعَة shamʿa Candle
جَريدَة jareeda Newspaper	هاتِف haatif Phone	خُضار ḳhoḍaar Vegetables	فاكِهة faakiha Fruit
سَفينة safeena Ship	ساحِل saaḥil Coast	طُيور ṭoyoor Birds	تَمام tamaam That's great/ok
رِحْلَة riḥla Journey/Trip	قِطار qiṭaar Train	وَرَقَة waraqa Paper	مِفْتاح miftaaḥ Key
مُغامَرَة moghamara Adventure	سَفَر safar Traveling	سَريع sareeʿ Fast	حَديقَة ḥadeeqa Garden/Park

Additional Practice:

حِكْمَة ḩikma Wisdom	بِنْت bint Girl	جَوارِب jawaarib Socks	حاسوب ḩaasoob Computer
سَعادَة sa'ada Happiness	سُكَّر sokkar Sugar	أسَد asad Lion	لَوْحَة lawḩa Portrait
خُروج ķhorooj Exiting	إمْرَأة imra-a Woman	سُمْسُم somsom Sesame	بَحْر baḩr Sea
إبْداع ibdaa' Creativity	سَلام salaam Peace	حَقيبَة ḩaqeeba Bag	بِرْكَة birka Pool
تَحَدّي taḩaddee Challenge	جَمال jamaal Beauty	سِكّين sikkeen Knife	نَجْمَة najma Star
تَأْخير ta-ķheer Delay	صَديق ṣadeeq Friend	قَلْب qalb Heart	جَبَل jabal Mountain
سُرْعَة sor'a Speed	رَفيق rafeeq Companion	مَطَر maţar Rain	قَميص qamees Shirt
رُجوع rojoo' Return	شَجاعَة shaja'a Bravery	حَلْوى ḩalwa Candy	فُسْتان fostaan Dress
فَوْز fawz Victory	فَرَح faraḩ Joy	بَطيء baţee Slow	خاتِم ķhaatim Ring

Stay Connected & Continue Your Arabic Journey!

◆ Your learning doesn't stop here! Connect with me on social media for more Arabic lessons, insights, and exclusive content:

- YouTube: Learn Arabic @Step-By-StepArabic
- TikTok: @stepbysteparabic
- Instagram: @stepbystep_arabic
- Facebook: @Step-by-Step Arabic Academy
- Email: nbeshqoy@gmail.com

◆ Want to take your Arabic to the next level? Get my comprehensive textbook **Step-By-Step Arabic Language - Beginner and Intermediate Learning**, available for purchase on Amazon.

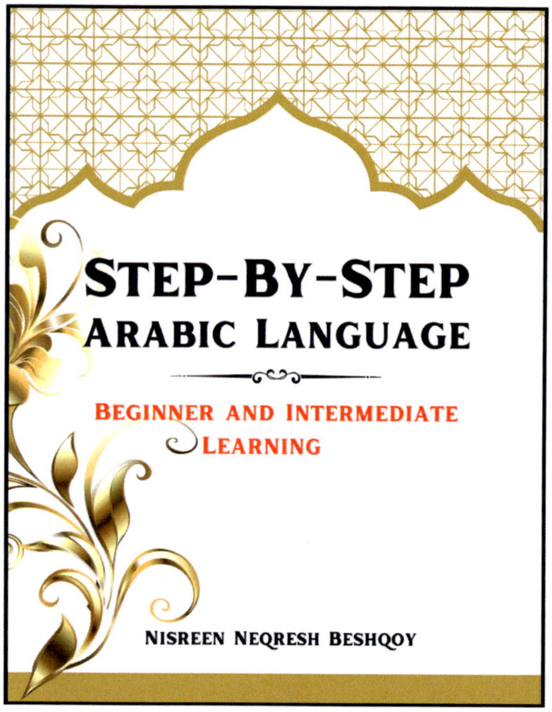

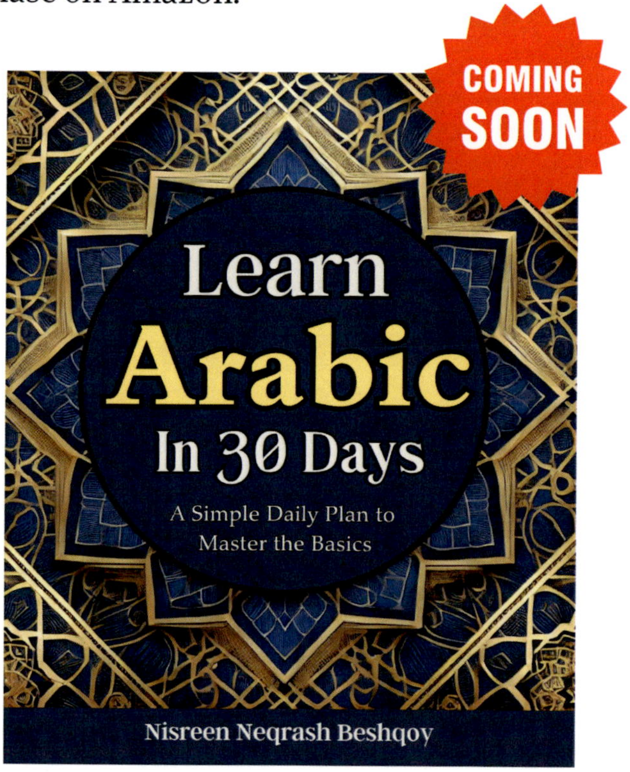

"Unlock the Beauty of the Arabic Language,
One Step at a Time."

-Professor Nisreen Beshqoy

www.ingramcontent.com/pod-product-compliance
Lightning Source LLC
Chambersburg PA
CBRC090837120626
46551CB00008B/689